Understanding
Girl
Bullying

and What to Do
About It

This book is dedicated to Bailey, Kennedy, Karlena, Meredith Julia,
and Mason. We hope you grow to be joyful, confident, secure, loving people.

Understanding
Girl
Bullying

and What to Do About It

Strategies to Help Heal the Divide

Julaine E. Field
Jered B. Kolbert
Laura M. Crothers
Tammy L. Hughes

CORWIN
A SAGE Company

For information:

Corwin
A SAGE Company
2455 Teller Road
Thousand Oaks, California 91320
(800) 233-9936
Fax: (800) 417-2466
www.corwinpress.com

SAGE Ltd.
1 Oliver's Yard
55 City Road
London EC1Y 1SP
United Kingdom

SAGE India Pvt. Ltd.
B 1/I 1 Mohan Cooperative
    Industrial Area
Mathura Road, New Delhi 110 044
India

SAGE Asia-Pacific Pte. Ltd.
33 Pekin Street #02-01
Far East Square
Singapore 048763

Printed in the United States of America.

Library of Congress Cataloging-in-Publication Data

Understanding girl bullying and what to do about it : strategies to help heal the divide / Julaine E. Field . . . [et al.].
    p. cm.
Includes bibliographical references and index.
ISBN 978-1-4129-6487-6 (cloth)
ISBN 978-1-4129-6488-3 (pbk.)

   1. Bullying in schools—United States. 2. Girls—Violence against—United States—Prevention. 3. Violence in women—United States—Prevention. I. Field, Julaine E.

LB3013.32.U63 2009
371.5′8—dc22   2008055974

This book is printed on acid-free paper.

11   12   13   14   15   10   9   8   7   6   5   4   3   2

Acquisitions Editor:	Jessica Allan
Editorial Assistant:	Joanna Coelho
Production Editor:	Eric Garner
Copy Editor:	Jeannette McCoy
Typesetter:	C&M Digitals (P) Ltd.
Proofreader:	Charlotte Waisner
Indexer:	Judy Hunt
Cover Designer:	Lisa Riley
Graphic Designer:	Rose Storey

Contents

List of Tables and Figures

LIST OF FIGURES

LIST OF TABLES

Acknowledgments

W e would like to thank the countless clients, students, and families who have invited us into their lives to hear their stories and to "walk with them" as they take steps toward change. We are humbled by their courage to explore the messiness of relationships—to feel the anxiety, pain, anger, and frustration involved in being honest while engaged in conflict. To our female students and clients, we respect your willingness to take risks and speak out about a challenging issue that many suggest is merely a part of girlhood. We thank you for your insights in helping to generate approaches to help counter and emotionally manage the consequences of the rather complex issue of relational aggression.

We would specifically like to thank the generous students, teachers, and administrators at Valley High School for allowing us to do some of our initial research to explore this issue. We would also like to acknowledge the wonderful seventh- and eighth-grade girls at Laurel Junior/Senior High School and Michelle McClelland, school counselor extraordinaire, who participated in the pilot of the Goodwill Girls curriculum. Also, a special thank you goes to the peer reviewers who took the time to review our manuscript and make it stronger:

Jennifer Betters
School Counselor
Verona School District
Verona, WI

Carol Dahir
Associate Professor of Counselor Education
New York Institute of Technology
New York, NY

Deborah Hardy
Chairperson of Guidance
Irvington School District
Irvington NY

Philip Kavanagh
District Guidance Director
Lakeland Central School District
Shrub Oak, NY

James L. Moore III
Associate Professor, Counselor Education
Coordinator, School Counseling Program
Director, Todd Anthony Bell National Resource Center on the African
    American Male
The Ohio State University
Columbus, OH

Tricia Peña
Principal
Cienega High School
Vail, AZ

Julia V. Taylor
Author of *Salvaging Sisterhood* and *G.I.R.L.S.*
(*Girls in Real Life Situations: Group Counseling Activities for Enhancing
    Social and Emotional Development*)
Professional School Counselor
Wake County Public Schools
Raleigh, NC

Finally, a heartfelt thank-you to our beautiful families, friends, and mentors whose support, encouragement, creativity, and kindness enrich our lives every day.

About the Authors

 **Julaine E. Field**, PhD, LPC, is an associate professor in the Department of Counseling and Development at Slippery Rock University of Pennsylvania. Dr. Field is a Licensed Professional Counselor (LPC) in Pennsylvania and currently works at a crisis shelter that serves victims of domestic violence and sexual assault. Her previous counseling experience includes working as a school counselor, mental health counselor, college counselor, and in private practice. She teaches graduate courses in the areas of group counseling, youth counseling, human sexuality, and courses related to school counseling. Dr. Field obtained her doctorate at North Carolina State University in Raleigh, NC. Dr. Field has authored publications related to counselor advocacy, gender identity, and relational and social aggression and has presented at international, national, and state conferences. She is involved in various women's initiatives on her campus and surrounding community.

 **Jered B. Kolbert**, PhD, LPC, is an associate professor in the Department of Counseling and Development at Slippery Rock University of Pennsylvania. Dr. Kolbert is a certified school counselor and LPC in Pennsylvania, and he is a National Certified Counselor (NCC). Dr. Kolbert teaches graduate-level courses in counseling, including family counseling, life-span development, school counseling practicum, and a professional orientation course for school counselors. He has also taught at the College of William and Mary in Virginia and Virginia Commonwealth University. Dr. Kolbert obtained his doctorate in counseling from the College of William and Mary, Williamsburg, Virginia. He has worked as a school counselor, marriage and family counselor, and substance abuse counselor. Dr. Kolbert has authored publications in nationally refereed journals on a variety of topics, including evolutionary psychology, bullying, relational aggression, gender identity, and moral development.

 **Laura M. Crothers**, DEd, is an associate professor in the school psychology program in the Department of Counseling, Psychology, and Special Education at Duquesne University, Pittsburgh, Pennsyvania. A New Jersey, Pennsylvania, and nationally certified school psychologist, Dr. Crothers has been recognized as a national expert in childhood bullying by the National Association of School Psychologists. She teaches the graduate-level consultation seminars in school psychology at Duquesne University and has taught courses in counseling, development, and educational psychology at Indiana University of Pennsylvania and Slippery Rock University. Dr. Crothers has contributed to the source literature by studying bullying in children and adolescents and is currently investigating the effects of job stress and locus of control upon teachers' behavior management styles, assisting teachers in managing student behavior problems in the classroom, using guidance curricular techniques to manage female adolescent peer aggression, and bullying of lesbian, gay, bisexual, and transgender youth. In addition to her scholarly writing, Dr. Crothers has delivered lectures and conducted presentations regionally, nationally, and internationally. Dr. Crothers provides professional reviews of manuscripts for the *Communiqué, School Psychology Review*, the *Trainers' Forum*, and the *Journal of Research in Rural Education*.

 **Tammy L. Hughes**, PhD, is an associate professor at Duquesne University, Pittsburgh, Pennsylvania and president of the Division of School Psychology of the American Psychological Association (APA). She is also the cochair of the School Psychology Leadership Roundtable (SPLR) and is a past-president of Trainers of School Psychologists (TSP). Dr. Hughes is an associate editor for *Psychology in the Schools* and serves on the editorial board of *School Psychology Quarterly* and *International Journal of Offender Therapy and Comparative Criminology*. She is the author and coauthor of numerous books, journal articles, chapters, and other publications on child violence, differentiating emotional disturbance and social maladjustment, and understanding the relationship between emotional dysregulation and conduct problems in children. She routinely provides scholarly presentations at national and international conferences and professional sessions for local and state constituents. Her work experience includes assessment, counseling, and consultation services in forensic and juvenile justice settings focusing on parent-school-interagency treatment planning and integrity monitoring.

Introduction

Adolescent friendships serve many purposes. They provide a social support network in the midst of biological, physical, and emotional changes. Friends commonly create a sphere of influence, a touchstone from which adolescents can assess their own attributes in relation to their peers. They are sources of information, advice, reassurance, and compassion. Friendships can motivate young people to find social strategies to fit in or belong in their desired peer group, which may include experimenting with or actually changing one's beliefs, behaviors, or appearance. Pipher (1994) writes, "Adolescents are travelers, far from home with no native land, neither children nor adults" (p. 52). Finally, adolescent friendships are often a safety net as adolescents "wander" toward adulthood, experimenting with aspects of their identity and conquering the process of moving away from the influence of parents and toward their own sense of identity.

Reliable teen friendships are invaluable in navigating the angst, terror, joys, and triumphs of adolescent life; however, when these friendships are not dependable, teens can find themselves adrift in challenging waters without the lifeboat of trustworthy friends. Taylor, Gilligan, & Sullivan (1995) writes that for girls, relationships can "encourage them when their courage falters and teach them strategies for dealing with adversity in the world. Yet relationships can also be an equally powerful hindrance if they become the source of discouragement or ridicule" (p. 174). In recent years, relational and social aggression, or bullying, among girls and female adolescents has gained national attention as a psychological issue worth exploring. Parents, educators, counselors, and extended family may be baffled at the psychological and emotional power friendships have over girls. Additionally, the threat of losing these friendships can feel overwhelming to teens. When these peer connections are in jeopardy, particularly for girls, the process of surveying the damage, fixing the problem, and monitoring the results can be all consuming. Furthermore, as caring adults watch the highs and lows, twists and turns in the course of adolescent friendships, many may struggle to identify ways to help girls or adolescent females cope when they experience conflict with their friends.

Gaining insight into the nature of conflict among girls provides adolescents and adults with awareness of how tension among friends or peers may take shape and why resolution is often elusive. Popular books such as *Odd Girl Out: The Hidden Culture of Aggression in Girls* (Simmons, 2002) and *Queenbees and Wannabes: Helping Your Daughter Survive Cliques, Gossip, Boyfriends and the Realities of Adolescence* (Wiseman, 2002) opened the doors for adolescent females to name or identify bullying, learn about its dynamics, understand its impact, and create strategies for managing peer conflict. Additionally, the popular adolescent movie, *Mean Girls* (2004), focuses on the dynamics involved in relational and social aggression among adolescent females in a school setting; although several other movies feature storylines or scenes that involve female characters in conflict, often being particularly nasty, rude, or indifferent to one another. For some, there is comedic value in featuring girls, who are "supposed" to be nice and kind, being covertly or overtly ruthless in how they solve problems with one another. For some adolescent females, these media representations confirm their peer experiences, providing validation for the role of victim or perpetrator. Unfortunately, Coyne, Archer, and Eslea (2004) found that viewing relational or socially aggressive approaches to conflict on television can increase the probability of using these behaviors in real life. Furthermore, "indirect/relational/social aggression is often portrayed on television to be justified, rewarded, and by attractive characters, all characteristics that have been shown to increase the likelihood that viewers will behave aggressively after viewing aggression on television" (p. 296).

In a recent article, three of the four authors of this book (Crothers, Field, & Kolbert, 2005) examined gender role, or how young people go about "being female," as one variable in explaining why girls may adapt and maintain behaviors associated with bullying. We found that gender role can contribute to self-reported relational aggression as participants "identified with a more traditional feminine gender role were more likely to perceive themselves as using relational aggression than were adolescent girls who identified with a nontraditional gender role" (p. 353). Males can exhibit relational and social aggression too; however, this book will primarily focus on bullying among females, as we believe that girls possess a different orientation (i.e., more emotional intensity) toward friendships than males, and socially sanctioned gender roles for girls may contribute directly to why girls engage in relational and social aggression more than physical aggression. Letendre (2007) writes, "girls' sense of themselves is deeply intertwined with connection to others and thus threatened when faced with situations where there is conflict or disagreement" (p. 356).

The purpose of this book is to blend academic, empirical, and practical perspectives to answer the questions of what relational and social aggression is, why it happens, what it looks like behaviorally, how to measure it, and what counselors, teachers, and parents can do to help girls and adolescent females with these issues. Furthermore, we will not distinguish between race, ethnicity, nationality, or socioeconomic status when discussing bullying among females, as we believe these behaviors can occur across different identities and worldviews. For example, in a study spanning seven different countries, Eslea et al. (2003) found that "bullying is a universal phenomenon with serious social and emotional correlates for the victims" (p. 80). Additionally, other studies have demonstrated that relational and social aggression has been identified across diverse cultural groups (Weisz et al. 1993; French, Jansen, & Pidada, 2002; Xie, Farmer, & Cairns, 2003). Österman et al. (1998) found evidence of indirect aggression across multiple racial and ethnic groups and concluded "indirect aggression is the most applied aggressive style among adolescent females in school settings" (p. 4). Thoroughly delineating how bullying is manifested among girls from different cultural backgrounds warrants additional research and another book.

This book is primarily written for counselors who work in schools, although school psychologists, teachers, administrators, mental health counselors, community counselors, and parents of girls may find the content useful to their respective practices or interests. Schools are the primary gathering place for young people and certainly may be a haven for bullying behavior. Our assumption is that counselors who work in schools should be invested in assisting students with issues that interfere with academic achievement. This interference includes an inability to focus one's attention on academic and healthy social development. If a young woman's psychological, emotional, and physical safety needs in her learning environment are not being met, she will not be able to thrive or reach her potential.

Finally, this book is not intended to further perpetuate any stereotypes that girls are mean, shallow, superficial, or incapable of getting along with one another. Through our clinical work in schools, mental health agencies, and our various research endeavors with females, each of us has directly observed the strength, intellect, and resilience of girls and adolescent females and their capacity to grow, evolve, change, and adapt. When girls engage in relational and social aggression, their "meanness" is not a static state or evidence that girls have a permanent inability to relate to one another in honest, assertive, or genuine terms. Rather, these behaviors signify that girls and adolescent females have not found alternative ways to resolve conflict, deal with female competition, garner peer acceptance, and find self-confidence. Furthermore, use of bullying also implies that girls have found what works while balancing society's expectations for female behavior with their own needs for expressing or repressing anger, frustration, and experiencing power.

This book will focus on what counselors can do to support adolescent females who experience and/or perpetrate relational or social aggression and help them learn alternative ways of managing conflict. Additionally, because school is a primary setting for all types of bullying, including relational and social aggression, this book also outlines what counselors can do to consult with teachers and parents whose students or children are impacted by relational and social aggression.

Chapter 1 defines relational and social aggression as well as suggests theoretical explanations for why it exists. The "rules of engagement" are presented to provide adults with further insight into how bullying works and may be experienced by females.

Chapter 2 focuses on assessment or measuring incidences of relational and social aggression within the school environment. School personnel are more likely to receive administrative support to develop and implement programming to address relational and social aggression among students if they are able to quantitatively (statistics) and qualitatively (description of problem) assess the need. Additionally, measuring the effectiveness of such programming may help to maintain funding or support.

Chapter 3 focuses on how relational and social aggression impacts the school climate and outlines different types of interventions that can be used in schools to address these issues at multiple levels.

Chapter 4 provides specific suggestions for counselors working with parents and teachers. Practical strategies are discussed so that counselors may add more tools to their current consultation repertoire.

Finally, Chapter 5 presents one approach that counselors may use when intervening with girls who engage in and/or have been victimized by relational or social aggression. The Goodwill Girls small-group curriculum is designed to help school counselors educate adolescent females about bullying while providing them with a constructive outlet to discuss these issues and try out new ways to relate to one another and resolve conflict. Because this curriculum was piloted with seventh- and eighth-grade girls in the fall of 2007 by one of the authors, each group lesson is followed by specific group facilitation tips for the counselor. Additionally, if group counseling is not feasible, each of the lessons could also be used as a series of classroom guidance lessons.

It is our hope that this book assists counselors with healing the divide among girls who have experienced or are experiencing relational and social aggression among their friendships or peer circles. We believe that female friendships hold magical holding and healing powers across the lifespan. No life obstacles are unconquerable when surrounded by caring, loving friends. Dismantling the impact and/or use of relational and social aggression early in a girl's life will assist her with learning to trust and relate to others honestly and assertively while she works through problems thoughtfully and constructively. These are skills that she will use throughout her lifetime.

Understanding Relational and Social Aggression

1

"Some girls are like mean but nice. They will be nice to your face, but then they will go say how much they hate 'her' or how annoying she is. But I think it hurts more if you say it behind their back than if you say it to their face because they gotta know the truth."

—R., 14 years old

"I know a lot of girls that like just get spiteful when they get mad. They get real spiteful and deceiving because they got mad at them and then they will regret it like two days later. Most of the time they don't get physical—they do something verbal. They will go around and tell something somebody said, or they will make it up and go around saying things just to get the person mad."

—B., 14 years old

"Stand up for each other. In order to show yourself as a true friend, you can stand up for one of your friends if they are having trouble with somebody. The only way to keep them so that they can trust you more is to stand up for them and let them know you will always be there for them."

—C., 14 years old

"Mostly, girls like to fight. I mean, girls are vicious. I mean boys, they don't really care. Boys—they can get in a fight one day and the next day they are like 'Aw, sorry about yesterday,' and 'Aw, that's all right—who cares.' Girls they just go after each other. They want to rip each other's hair out."

—A., 13 years old

> "You don't really purposely want to do that [relational aggression] to someone unless—like you are really mean. But it is really much easier to be nice to people because it comes out easier."
>
> —A., 14 years old
> (Middle school participants in a
> Goodwill Girls Group, Fall 2007)

Over the last two decades, interest in bullying among school-age children and how these behaviors impact the development of both the victims and perpetrators has increased among educators and researchers. Bullying is typically thought of as aggressive physical or verbal assaults against a "weaker" person so that the bully can gain power over that individual or social status among his or her peers. Olweus (2003), a leading author in bullying research and intervention, defines a bully as an individual who intentionally attempts to inflict physical or psychological harm on another person through proactive, overt aggression. Furthermore, bullies often note the imbalance of strength (i.e., this person will not defend herself) as a rationale to victimize a particular person. However, as multiple researchers (e.g., Feshbach, 1969; Crick, 1996; Grotpeter & Crick, 1996; Archer & Coyne, 2005) have noted, including Olweus, bullying can appear different than its traditional definition when practiced in a covert manner, emphasizing emotional or relational harm rather than threat of or actual physical harm. A covert approach limits detection by overseeing adults or the victim themselves at times and may actually do more harm to the victim if her social connections and reputation with others are of particular importance. Furthermore, indirect forms of aggression also allow the perpetrator to "appear" amiable while secretly orchestrating an attack on another person.

DEFINITIONS OF RELATIONAL
AND SOCIAL AGGRESSION

Indirect aggression (similar to relational and social aggression) was first defined by Feshbach in 1969 in order to explain covert aggressive behavior (e.g., spreading rumors, giving someone the silent treatment, or isolating someone from the group) versus overt aggressive behavior (e.g., kicking, hitting, screaming, threatening, name calling in front of victim). Indirect aggression was first examined by a Finnish group (Lagerspetz, Björkqvist, & Peltonen, 1988) who found that a unique identifying feature of this form of aggression is that the bully could remain anonymous because of the underground nature of the aggression, allowing the perpetrator to give the appearance of innocence. In turn, perpetrators avoid detection by the victim or adults who may be monitoring them. Indirect aggression is now commonly referred to as relational or social aggression in the literature. Researchers such as Crick and Grotpeter (1995), Crick (1996), Crick and Grotpeter (1996), Crick et al. (1999), and Coyne, Archer, and Eslea (2006) have explored the formal definitions of relational and social aggression as well as how to measure the impact on victims, perpetrators, victim/perpetrators, and bystanders. Additionally, other scholarly articles have explored incidences of relational and social aggression among school-aged children and its impact on school climate (Merrell, Buchanan, & Tran, 2006). Several researchers (e.g., Crick & Grotpeter, 1995; Owens, Shute, & Slee, 2000; Hayward & Fletcher, 2003) have found that girls are more likely to be relationally aggressive than boys; girls rate the use of relational aggression more favorably than boys (Crick & Werner, 1998), and yet girls are more likely to view relational aggression and verbal aggression as more harmful to themselves than boys (Coyne, Archer, & Eslea, 2006).

Researchers hold differing opinions in how to define relational and social aggression. A recent article by Archer and Coyne (2005) attempts to clarify if relational aggression and social aggression are the same phenomenon or if the two terms actually describe separate sets of behaviors. *Relational aggression* is commonly defined as behaviors that intend to harm a person's friendships or feelings of belonging in a particular peer group (Crick & Grotpeter, 1995). Specific behaviors may include withdrawing one's friendship out of anger, isolating a person from a peer group, spreading rumors about a person to damage her reputation, and ultimately causing peer rejection. The goal is often to punish a girl or adolescent female for a perceived friendship "violation" that calls into question her loyalty to a friend. A female friend can be deemed disloyal by talking or flirting with a friend's boyfriend, not sticking up for a friend if she is being talked about by someone else, and the appearance of being unkind—such as questioning a friend's decision making, appearance, or behavior. This relational "punishing" for a friendship infraction can feel excruciating because the girl being punished may not understand what she did or who she did it to if enough people in her friendship group are acting angry and isolating her from the group. Indeed a girl may feel that everyone is angry with her, and if the perpetrator has enough social power and influence over other peers, the perpetrator may have gained several allies for the shunning and punishment process. Participating in the punishment, even if they themselves are not angry with the victim, allows the followers to gain a sense of cohesiveness with others (e.g., "We are angry with her"), which may enhance their social standing and ensure that they are not the immediate targets.

For example, if Joanna was seen talking to Rashida's boyfriend in the hallway before lunch, and it appeared that Joanna was flirting with him, spectators on their way to lunch may then relay this information back to Rashida. If Rashida is quick to respond with anger, she may immediately withdraw from Joanna (e.g., move to a different lunch table), talk to her other friends about Rashida's friendship violation (e.g., telling everyone within earshot that Joanna is after her boyfriend), and garner the support of other girls (e.g., "Joanna may try this with your boyfriend. We can't trust her."), who will now help in punishing Joanna. Because no one has actually communicated with Joanna about why Rashida originally became angry, Joanna, if troubled by this treatment from Rashida and other recruited "help," may feel responsible for investigating what happened and trying to fix the friendship problem. This entire scenario could occur in a very short period of time. Joanna's afternoon may seem ruined as she tries to unravel what occurred to cause the treatment that she is receiving. Furthermore, technology such as instant messaging, texting, or calling using cell phones can easily move the conflict from school to the girls' homes. An absence of messages or calls, if the girl is being cut off from the group, can feel just as painful as messages or calls that are accusatory or angry.

Social aggression has been defined by some to describe those behaviors that seek to harm a person's social status through attacking her social or sexual reputation. This may include demeaning her physical appearance, questioning her decisions—or any other aspect of her—revealing her secrets to others, accusing her of trying to be "better than" others, or simply making up stories to tell about her that will cause her reputation to be in question. If the attacks are vicious enough, they may seem to question her very worth as a human being. Social aggression may include behaviors such as verbal confrontations to embarrass someone, repeatedly putting someone down, making a game of belittling someone, eye-rolling and other negative nonverbal forms of communication, spreading rumors to compromise a girl's place in the social hierarchy (i.e., jeopardizing popularity with slurs about sexual reputation), or socially excluding a girl from a social group or groups. Although this definition sounds similar to relational aggression, one difference is that relational aggression may occur as a result of a specific conflict between individuals who identify as friends; however, social aggression may occur in a larger social circle due to jealousy of peers, perceived female competition for attention or boyfriends, to gain social status or power among peers by lowering someone's standing in the social hierarchy, or for entertainment purposes. In 2005, we conducted a qualitative study in a high school in which adolescent females were asked to explain why a group of girls would socially ostracize a particular girl. The respondents stated that this behavior may be born of envy or jealousy, competing for social status, need for fun or entertainment, or to deflect the potential or possibility of them receiving negative peer attention (Crothers, Field, & Kolbert, 2005).

Social aggression is illustrated in the following scenario. Brianna is a fifteen-year-old female who is sitting in study hall working on her biology homework. Because she is struggling with the content, she is focused on finishing her homework and preparing for a test later that afternoon. Simultaneously, she is trying to ignore the giggling behind her. She is a sophomore dating a senior basketball player, Marcus, who broke up with Samantha, a popular senior, who sits three rows behind her in study hall. Silently, a girl sitting next to her, leans in close and drops a letter on Brianna's desk. She opens it to find the following:

Dear B:

Just so you know, no one is impressed with you or your bullshit. We are tired of you acting like you are better than everyone else.

We know the truth—you are a whore, and Marcus will figure that out soon enough.

Forty people had signed the letter. Needless to say, Brianna is stunned by this letter and unsure of what to do next.

Obviously, technology can exacerbate social aggression and allows it to infiltrate a girl's home and family environment, which may include receiving anonymous emails or text messages or receiving mean emails from a friend's email as the result of someone else using the account. On the other hand, this can also occur to signify to a girl that a close confidant has been "turned" by the larger peer group and has joined in the circle of perpetrators. Finally, Web pages or Youtube postings can be created for the sole purpose of publicly disgracing a person being pinpointed by a group. Victims may understandably feel both helpless and humiliated with such exposure.

CYBERBULLYING

Debate continues as to whether the terms *relational aggression* and *social aggression* are broad enough or specific enough to describe all covert and overt behaviors that involve psychological or emotional bullying. What can be agreed upon is that this type of bullying, although not physically harmful, can wreak havoc with a girl's emotional stability and sense of belonging within her peer group. To complicate the definitions further, cyberbullying must also be considered in this discussion as girls and adolescent females are plugged in to various forms of technology for socializing purposes. *Cyberbullying* is defined as "the use of electronic technology to deliberately harass or intimidate; unlike the schoolyard bully of yesteryear, the cyberbully can hide behind online anonymity and attack around the clock, invading the privacy of a teen's home" (Long, 2008, p. 28). Because of widespread use of technology and the tendency for adolescents to be "plugged in" whenever possible, relational and social aggression can occur from remote locations at all hours, making the feasibility of escaping the torment extremely difficult. Turning off one's computer may seem a difficult choice if an adolescent female's support system is simultaneously "present" where the bullies linger.

In a recent study involving 4,000 middle school students, 18% stated that they had been bullied online in the last two months (CQ Researcher, 2008). Other reports indicate that the percentage is actually closer to one in three students recently being targeted online by students using cyberbullying. Tragically, the impact of cyberbullying can be overwhelming for adolescents. In July of 2008, the state of Missouri passed a law that outlaws cyberbullying (AP, 2008). This law came into existence after a 13-year-old girl, Megan Meier, committed suicide in 2006 after receiving mean, distressing messages online from a teenager named "Josh." Josh was actually an adult woman and mother of a teenage girl with whom Megan had had a rocky friendship. Using the identity of Josh, a supposed sixteen-year-old boy who Megan thought she was developing a relationship with, this mother engaged in relational aggression through a false identity via a MySpace page. If others would have joined in the taunting, this would certainly meet the definition of social aggression via the Internet. In conclusion, it is worth speculating that individuals may be more ruthless online because they are not in the physical presence of their target, the human being who they can see actually see or hear.

Just as cyberbullying can have devastating consequences for victims, there is empirical evidence to suggest that the social and emotional development of perpetrators and victims of relational and social aggression may be hindered. Girls more than males report that relational and social aggression is more damaging to their friendships, and girls are also more likely to report a "shake up" in self-confidence when they are victims of relational aggression (Goldstein & Tisak, 2004). Victims of relational and social aggression are more likely to experience internalizing symptoms (e.g., anxiety and sadness) and lower overall self-worth. Furthermore, those who experience multiple forms of aggression (e.g., covert and overt) are more likely to experience maladaptive social and emotional development (Prinstein, Boergers, & Vernberg, 2001) and distress (Crick & Grotpeter, 1996). Perpetrators of relational and social aggression are, over time, more likely to be depressed (Prinstein et al., 2001), anxious (Loukas, Paulos, & Robinson, 2005) lonely (Crick & Grotpeter, 1995) and abuse substances (Sullivan, Farrell, & Kliewer, 2006).

WHY USE RELATIONAL AND SOCIAL AGGRESSION?

"A lot of people are two-faced, and girls are like that. They don't want to cause trouble with that person, but they will go around talking about it because they like don't have the courage to actually stand up for themselves or say it to their face."

—C., 13 years old

"I think, like if you are mad at someone, then you go tell your friends about them. You are just letting all of your anger out 'cause you don't want to let your anger out on the person you are mad at . . . I don't know . . . 'cause you don't want them to hate you or be mad at you."

—J., 14 years old (Both were middle school participants in a Goodwill Girls group.)

Theoretical Perspectives on Why Girls May Use Relational or Social Aggression

✓ Evolutionary Psychology

✓ Systemic (Social and Cultural) Influences

✓ Social Learning

✓ Developmental

Why are girls relationally and socially aggressive with one another? This complex question cannot be easily answered, as many variables are at play. For example, girls may learn to be bullies because they are unconsciously or consciously competing with one another, have observed significant others (e.g., parent, teacher, aunt, or other significant adults) use these behaviors, or because they have not learned other ways of expressing anger and hurt that simultaneously get their needs for affiliation and close-ness with others met. Girls may also learn to become relationally and socially aggressive because they do not believe that it is okay to be straight-forward or assertive with one another, as girls and women in American society who demonstrate these tendencies are sometimes negatively labeled by observers. Terms such as "bossy" and "uppity" are rarely applied to males. The following discussion, although not exhaustive, examines rela-tional and social aggression from different theoretical angles, attempting to shed light on why girls or female adolescents may use these behaviors.

EVOLUTIONARY PSYCHOLOGY

In the book *Woman's Inhumanity to Woman*, Chesler (2001) suggests that there may be two main evolutionary explanations for why females may use bullying. Evolutional psychology explains that throughout our evolution-ary development, women are wired for emotional connections with others. For example, female infants are more likely to study human faces for emo-tions and respond to others based on emotional cues, plus female children are more likely to play collaboratively with others rather than competitively (Brizendine, 2006). Both are examples of how most females thrive on rela-tionships or connections with others. Brizendine (2006) writes that most females "prefer to avoid conflict because discord puts them at odds with their urge to stay connected, to gain approval and nurturance" (p. 21). Close relationships and staying connected to others has served the evolu-tionary purpose of safety as well as maintaining shelter, food, and having assistance with rearing children. In fact, gossip or the act of talking about others, when viewed through the perspective of needing close connections with others, may actually serve the purpose of creating intimacy, friend-ship, and connection with other females. On the other hand, awareness that relationships are important to other females creates a window of opportunity to attack a woman where it hurts the most. Emotional con-nections being valued by others and one's reputation within a social circle may all become part of the arsenal when girls do battle with one another.

Another explanation for relational and social aggression from an evolu-tionary psychology perspective is that once adolescence is reached, females, assuming heterosexuality, often feel the impulse to compete with other females for male attention. Although it may not register consciously, the female brain may be wired to do what it takes to make herself appear more attractive than other females in hopes of capturing the best mate possible (e.g., healthy, able to reproduce and provide for offspring). This serves the evolutionary purpose of assuring insemination by a quality male, thus helping to ensure the viability of an infant. Rising to the top of a social structure or group of eligible females from an evolutionary perspective may be accomplished through a female's physical appearance, fertility, exemplary nurturing skills, and/or her ability to strategically creating a climate (e.g., gossiping about another female's sexual reputation) where other females are less desirable. This competition for a mate ultimately results in females doing battle with one another in ways that harm another's reputation while not using overt bullying, thus harming their own. The reason the behaviors must be covert is to avoid being inconsistent with a female gender role or the appearance of being nurturing. Appearing kind and amiable while strategically cutting off or shunning a woman from a group allows a female to maneuver socially among the possible mates and among her competition. Chesler (2001) writes, "As most women know, a woman can make life hell, on a moment-by-moment basis, for any other woman she envies, fears, or with whom she must compete for resources" (pp. 36–37).

This phenomenon may be observed when a new female is brought into a social circle. For example, if a female adolescent enters a high school as a new student, other females may feel threatened by her as she may have the potential to disrupt the hierarchy of popularity and social power among her female classmates and compete for someone's boyfriend. This phenomenon is particularly true for females who may lack self-confidence, unfortunately an all too common occurrence during adolescence, or find a core sense of their identity through whom they date. If the new female is deemed competitive by her appearance, social intelligence, talents, capacity to make friends, or ability to garner attention from male classmates, she may become the target of social aggression in hopes of diminishing her social foothold or popularity among her peers. Her reputation may be challenged, and she may endure harsh treatment from other females.

What is difficult about this particular explanation for bullying is that the impetus for behaving in this manner is largely unconscious. Adolescent females may not be able to explain why they dislike a new girl at school or why it seems appropriate to attack her socially. Furthermore, while following a strict line of evolutionary reasoning, openly discussing the idea that an adolescent female has an innate impulse to compete with other females for the best possible mate who stands the greatest chance of impregnating her for propagation of the species and providing for her and her offspring will seem ridiculous in our modern age. However, many girls or adolescent females may be willing to consciously entertain the idea that they compete with one another. One of the best strategies for appearing "great" is to make someone else appear "awful." Fortunately, talking about this sense of competition openly and reviewing the costs (e.g., closeness with other females) can assist young women in making alternative choices.

SYSTEMIC (SOCIAL AND CULTURAL) INFLUENCES

Over the last forty years, the United States has experienced a loosening of gender-role expectations for females. Girls have more options than ever before and are easily able to identify powerful, influential women who have realized achievements of historical significance. However, despite this progress and broadening of career, economic, educational, and athletic opportunities, females still receive mixed messages about how to *be* female and what behaviors are considered feminine. Gender-role socialization or how girls learn to be female at the micro (e.g., family, school) and macro (e.g., media) levels of society may contribute to why females distrust one another, exercise emotional distance with one another, and participate in social and relational aggression.

For example, if girls are supposed to be nice, kind, and able to always exercise self-control to meet societal expectations for acceptable femininity, this will constrict their ability to express anger and frustration. When these normal emotions are restricted, often times out of fear of losing a particular relationship or appearing unkind in front of significant others, girls may have difficulty finding the means to express these emotions constructively or work through problems to healthy resolution. Despite more progressive gender roles in the United States, an assertive woman is still often labeled a "bitch" where a male counterpart, exercising the same behaviors, is labeled "strong" or a "leader." Female children may be told to "play nice" or "talk it out" when a conflict emerges among friends; however, boys may be given the freedom to openly have conflict in a rough and tumble way, demonstrating masculinity while being given an endorsement of "boys being boys." On the other hand, some females who are aggressive with one another may receive attention for the aggression, adding to a "cat fight" mentality, which is entertaining for some and portrays women as enemies. For example in July 2008, Danika Patrick, driver in the Indy Racing League, had a verbal altercation with another female driver. This incident stole the headlines for the Ohio race making who actually won the race inconsequential. National publicity for an argument between two attractive female Indy car drivers highlights interest in female competition and aggression; some consider it almost sexual in nature. Additionally, this type of national coverage may promote this type of behavior because of the attention that may be received. Unfortunately, this behavior reinforces the stereotype of women viewing other women as enemies or individuals with whom to compete.

On the macro level, entertainers such as Britney Spears, Jessica Simpson, Paris Hilton, and Lindsay Lohan have cashed in during various points of their careers by portraying shallow, superficial women obsessed with their own looks and sex appeal while downplaying their intelligence, independence, and strength. Despite excellent examples of how females may creatively combat "lookism" (e.g., the television show *Ugly Betty*), girls and adolescent females are still bombarded on a daily basis with media images suggesting what they should aspire to look like in order to be successful or well liked by others. If the societal and cultural focus is on feminine beauty, and appearance is a valuable social commodity, this may encourage girls to compete with each other in the beauty venue. For example, in the popular magazine *OK*, female celebrities are often pitted against one another in a pictorial competition if both are caught wearing the same designer outfit. With their photos side by side, fashion contributors decide who looks best in the outfit by calculating a percentage, and the woman with the highest percentage wins.

Girls and adolescent females can also compete through formal beauty pageants, bikini contests, homecoming or prom courts, on social networking pages on the Internet, or in other social settings. On a very basic level, girls understand the inherent day-to-day contest of who looks the best in school on a particular day or during a specific event. Hours of applying makeup, arranging hair, or assembling an outfit in the morning before school is symbolic of a girl's conscious or unconscious participation in the beauty competition. Being obsessed with their appearance and weight distracts girls, adolescent females, and women from other matters. Feminism suggests that traditional gender-role socialization for girls or acting in certain ways that are consistent with being appropriately female, including the mandate for beauty, helps to support patriarchy or a male-controlled society and institutions. If many females are insecure in their own skin or in how they appear to others, they are more likely to devote a great deal of time and energy to how they appear and less likely to be confident individuals.

In her book, *The Beauty Myth*, Naomi Wolf (2002) contends that competition and conflict among women must be addressed by women themselves for change to occur. Waiting for the media or other institutions to free women from the beauty mandate is hopeful thinking, as there is much to gain economically and socially, if some women remain distracted. Wolf states, "The toughest but most necessary change will come not from men or from the media but from women in the way we see and behave toward other women" (p. 283). Perpetual competition in the beauty venue distances women from one another and adds to an aura of distrust. In this type of climate, girls or adolescent females may view other girls as enemies until they prove themselves otherwise. In a 2005 study with adolescent females, research participants used terms such as "catty, backstabbing, judgmental, jealous, devious, manipulative, dramatic, and defensive"

(Crothers et al., 2005, p. 352) to describe their female peers. This finding begs the question as to what societal or cultural forces help to reinforce this type of thinking among girls. How do girls learn to think this way about one another? In Brown's (2003) book *Girlfighting,* she argues that rather than focusing on the competitive behavior of young women as overly problematic or pathological, more attention should be paid to the cultural forces that reinforce jealousy, mistrust, and competition for males' attention among girls. If girls can be distracted by battling one another, they are less likely to notice or have energy to address the systemic and institutional challenges that still face them.

SOCIAL LEARNING THEORY

According to Bandura (1977), social learning theory postulates that individuals learn to function in a social context based on observing and learning from others. When individuals in the immediate environment are reinforced for their behavior, an observing individual is more likely to emulate that behavior. For example, if an adolescent female observes a peer gossiping about another girl and the one initiating the gossip is popular, has many friends, and gains positive attention for spreading the rumors, this observing female will likely adopt this behavior according to social learning theory. Additionally, individuals who model their behavior after others in the environment are more likely to be accepted by their peers because they are acting in a predictable manner, using the behaviors that others use. Pipher (1994) writes, "girls are at risk of becoming the biggest enforcers and proselytizers for the culture" (p. 68). Practicing social and relational aggression may actually cause some girls to win the favor of others in their peer circles, even if only temporarily. Choosing to *not* play by the rules or social codes of (1) knowing which girl is in power, (2) following the powerful girl and allowing her to make decisions for others, or (3) participating in the shunning or punishing of a particular girl on a particular day, could result in the nonconforming female experiencing "social suicide" (Pipher, 1994, p. 68) or becoming the next victim of bullying. Adolescent girls who respond in predictable ways or social patterns through practicing social and relational aggression often are trying to please other girls within their peer circle, perpetuating the cycle of female bullying.

Finally, significant adults, including mothers, aunts, and grandmothers, may have created the original training ground for social and relational aggression within a family. Some girls, observing the influential women in their lives, may have learned that they are not to be open about discussing conflict with others. They may learn that avoiding conflict is the best course, therefore making it incredibly challenging to find resolution to some relational problems. Additionally, some girls may have learned to act nice to someone and then talk behind her back or "cut off" or isolate someone by not inviting her to an event and making sure the woman learns that she was excluded. Finally, some adults may also model how to threaten to withdraw from a relationship if the female counterpart is not following a prescribed formula for how to relate to one another. In a 2005 qualitative study, girls reported that their "tendency either to indirectly address or to avoid conflict was supported by adults" (Crothers et al., 2005, p. 353). Therefore, adult females may be unconsciously or consciously endorsing behaviors that lead to or reinforce bullying. If adult females are willing to examine their own approaches to conflict and competition with other females and model constructive behaviors for resolving differences, this would provide young women with exposure to alternatives to relational and social aggression.

DEVELOPMENTAL PERSPECTIVE

A broad range of coping skills is needed for young females to successfully navigate adolescence and adulthood while achieving a positive sense of self, healthy relationships, and hope and direction for one's future. Interestingly, just as female adolescents are experiencing tremendous shifts in their biological, emotional, intellectual, and physical growth, they are simultaneously separating psychologically from parents and moving toward peers for advice, support, and identification. In his stages of psychosocial development, Erik Erikson described this developmental passage as *identity versus role confusion* and believed that most females develop according to an interpersonal pattern (e.g., focus on relationships, emphasizing affiliation or connection to others), whereby males develop according to an intrapersonal pattern (e.g., focus on individual, personal success, competition with others) (Lytle, Bakken, & Romig, 1997). Because of the separation from parents, peers become the preferred socializing agents. Some adolescent females may adopt maladaptive behaviors or less desirable coping skills that nonetheless allow them to function in their social circles. For example, because their peers may gossip, some girls or adolescent females may begin to adopt this social practice to gain social status with peers, feel comfortable in social situations in which they are less familiar, and relieve themselves of undesirable feelings (e.g., social anxiety).

"Fitting in" with a desired peer group is important during the elementary years; however, it takes on even more significance during adolescence. Peer groups are often the most important social connection for teenagers. For some adolescent females, relational or social aggression is an automatic response to anger or conflict that allows them to react in a way that is predictable and consistent with how many peers respond to perceived provoking events and helps to alleviate their own anger and frustration. Incredibly, some adolescent females are not consciously aware that gossiping about someone is actually what they are doing to work through their anger.

If able to spend enough time with adolescent females, one is quickly able to discover that many are in conflict with others on a regular basis, which is in part due to them being in conflict with themselves. Because of the focus on identity development and the use of peers as a litmus test for one's own sense of self and success, questions such as, "Do I look good?" "Do people like me?" "Am I okay?" "What do they think about me?" and "How can I get them to like me?" can plague a young woman's thoughts and cause her to at times feel desperate, confused, and anxious to belong. While engaged in the process of worrying about these competing thoughts, it is often difficult to be patient, forgiving, and understanding of a peer whose less-than-sensitive behavior is driven by her own egocentrism and similar insecure thoughts. This internal conflict of wanting to be okay can also produce a hypersensitivity to actual or perceived criticism or negative appraisal by others.

For example, if a young woman takes the risk of answering a question in class and is shunned by the teacher for her response, and peers around her giggle because of this transaction, she may or may not be able to see humor in the situation and may instead believe that her friends are disloyal and making fun of her in a mean-spirited way. If this teenager is filled with self-doubt, she may quickly become angry about the situation and direct it toward her peers who may not have had negative intentions. Typically, an adolescent female will seek out a confidant to tell the story to and who will hopefully lend support. The moment she describes this scenario to the confidant and articulates anger toward the peers in her class, the person lending support ultimately decides whether to keep the friend's frustration in confidence and allow her to vent or transfer that information to others— using it as social information to stir up controversy ("She is really ticked at the girls in her math class today because . . .") or to gain social leverage ("Guess what I heard today? Call me later, and I will tell you!"). Carriers of secrets possess, even if momentarily, social power and prestige. They can receive attention by being sought after and confirming details of what she said about them. If the young woman in the scenario above were not self-conscious and could see the teacher's rudeness and her friends' amusement as separate from herself or not revealing anything about who *she* is, then the social outlet for anger is not needed. Therefore, relational and social aggression can certainly occur because of internal conflict and lack of self-confidence or ego strength. Fortunately, if girls are given the opportunity to engage in perspective taking with others, acknowledging that they may be quick to inaccurately judge a situation at times, they will learn critical thinking skills about their social environment.

WHAT DOES IT FEEL LIKE TO BE IN A RELATIONALLY AND SOCIALLY AGGRESSIVE CLIMATE?

The previous portion of this chapter has outlined potential explanations for why girls may use relational and social aggression with one another. It is only natural for counselors then to turn their attention to what they can do to intervene successfully. Additionally, parents and teachers may come to counselors seeking information about how to help their daughters or students. However, prior to learning how to intervene, it is important for adults to attempt to understand what it is like to be in a social climate where this type of bullying is used. Parents, teachers, and counselors may or may not be effective in their efforts to help because of the adult's inability to empathize with what a girl may be going through mentally and emotionally when faced with these issues. Advice such as, "Just ignore them!" "Get over it!" "It will pass, and they will pick on someone else soon," or "You know what they are saying is not true, so don't worry about it" may seem particularly unsupportive for a person whose friendships and social support are in the midst of a vanishing act. To assist adults in understanding the dynamics associated with bullying among girls and adolescent females, a military metaphor is used to explain the norms or unwritten, often unmentioned, rules of engagement. Although these norms are identifiable, it does not mean that they are inevitable or unalterable.

RULES OF ENGAGEMENT

Rule of Engagement 1: Be on Guard

In a setting where practices of relational and social aggression may abound (e.g., school), young women may feel the need to be on alert for any subtle change in peers' or associates' behavior that can be interpreted (accurately or inaccurately) as warning signs for an oncoming attack. This monitoring can cause high levels of anxiety, sensitivity, and reactivity when a perceived incident does occur. Culotta and Goldstein (2008) found that adolescent girls are more socially anxious and jealous than boys, perhaps due to their tendency to emphasize the importance of relationships and friendships. Feeling vulnerable to the moods of others can cause young women to feel anxious, irritable, and under pressure.

Rule of Engagement 2: Know the Ranks

Males and females, young and old understand that some individuals possess more power and influence than others, which may manifest as controlling what others will socially do or say. Among adolescent females, there is a social ranking or hierarchy that determines how much attention a person receives, how much others strive to be like this person, who this person will most likely date, and how easy it may be for her to rally the troops in support of her goals (e.g., to destroy the reputation of another girl). Adolescent girls often feel that they need to be aware of this ranking system and perhaps tread lightly while in the company of "generals" and "colonels" at their school.

Rule of Engagement 3: Camouflage Is Used for a Reason

Although many teens often desire a sense of independence and act in rebellious ways, fitting in with one's peer group is a mandate for teens who want broad social circles of support. Hair, clothing, shoes, hobbies, interests, and one's vernacular are all methods by which individuals may conform to trends in their peer group. Acting in ways that differentiate oneself from the crowd can cause an adolescent female to be more vulnerable to social attack, particularly if she is successful in some way that causes her to stand out from the crowd or garners a great deal of attention from males. This is where ranking can become confusing, as the socially awkward girl without trendy clothes and the homecoming queen can both be in jeopardy of being targeted by socially aggressive peers.

Rule of Engagement 4: Know Your Enemy

One of the most frustrating aspects of relational and social aggression is that the aggressor may remain undetected. For example, an adolescent female may begin to experience the cold shoulder from a circle of girls, and she may not know who initiated the attack or why. Therefore, it is often left up to the recipient of the attack to investigate the origin of the offensive. This may include asking others who appear close to or part of the circle of girls who are doing the ignoring or shunning. This investigation can often reveal troubling results, as the attack may have been launched due to faulty information, a miscommunication, or for fun. As stated previously, many females employ relational and social aggression as it allows them to appear kind and friendly to peers and outside observers as no observable attacking behaviors may be evident. Furthermore, if confronted, many perpetrators will pretend to not know what the victim is talking about or attempt to make the victim feel as if she has misunderstood what is happening.

Rule of Engagement 5: Prepare the Troops or "Fight When I Say Fight!"

When conflict is occurring among adolescent females, one is expected to go to battle alongside one's friends. This behavior is a testament to a friend's sense of loyalty to another and is expected. If a friend attempts to straddle the fence or not take sides, there may be repercussions after this particular battle is waged. Going to battle poses certain risks as the friend may become part of the ridicule, rumor mill, or silent treatment and not participating can cause that person to be seen as a traitor. A special weapon that can be used is enlisting male participants who will join a particular side and participate in battle. If males are on the attack, they may be willing to carry out more overt orders that can cause additional layers of embarrassment. For example, if a male soldier comments on a girl's weight or sexuality, it can feel especially devastating to the victim. Males may be willing to engage in such acts as they may win the social rewards of associating with the females in the highest ranks or circle of power.

Rule of Engagement 6: Treason May Be Likely

As soldiers are recruited to do battle, girls, who normally garner very little attention from others or who are low in rank, influence, and popularity, may capitalize on the opportunity to earn social status by becoming involved in the conflict by taking sides, relaying information back and forth, and manipulating the message to heighten the stakes and their own importance as a messenger. Treasonous individuals, who are often peripheral to the actual conflict, can fan the flame and interfere with resolving the conflict. Often, when girls (or students in general) participate in a mediation session to resolve a conflict, the counselor must first determine the main combatants and bring them together. After the conflict is worked through, a final step in the mediation process is to have the combatants inform their army that the battle is over and any additional action, whether it is spreading rumors, giving threatening looks, or talking badly about a person, should cease and desist.

Rule of Engagement 7:
Medals for Bravery May Not Be Honored

Unfortunately, girls who possess a firm set of personal boundaries and work to rise above the fray of interpersonal conflict may be at risk for heightened attacks. Bullying is often used because it works, meaning that those using these strategies often achieve the desired results. Inflicting relational and/or social harm to the point that a girl is publicly upset, walking on egg shells in attempt to comply, seeking help from authority figures, or avoiding social settings indicates that she is raising the white flag, and the attackers are victorious. Not responding in a predictable manner by being upset or influenced by relationally or socially aggressive acts can cause a surge by the individuals inflicting the attack, expanding the assault. It is sometimes helpful if the girl who deserves a purple heart knows ahead of time that her attackers may try harder to win before they give up the battle.

Rule of Engagement 8: Peace Treaties May Be Elusive

Because of the indirect nature of relational and social aggression, adolescent females may not participate in the direct expression of anger. In contrast to boys who may feel free to be angry and even physical with a peer (which often deescalates the conflict), females may not feel that there is an available peer or socially sanctioned avenue to deal directly with a person with whom they are in conflict. Furthermore, keeping one's frustration below the surface allows the young woman to maintain her public image of composure or innocence. Assertiveness skills may be in short supply if a young woman has not learned this approach to conflict resolution from her significant adults or if assertiveness is not reinforced. Furthermore, peace treaties may not be possible while females are actively competing for attention, popularity, and social status among peers.

CONCLUSION

There are various theoretical explanations that may help to explain why girls or adolescent females may use various bullying techniques. However, understanding why it exists is not nearly as important as knowing what it is and how it may compromise a girl's social and emotional development. Being familiar with the rules of engagement for relational and social aggression can assist adults in imagining the angst, confusion, anger, and frustration that may be experienced by girls or adolescent females while navigating their social climate. Furthermore, these rules may help to highlight for counselors and educators the types of behaviors to look for when monitoring a school climate for bullying. Measuring the incidences of relational or social aggression or assessing how this form of bullying is operationalized in a particular class, grade level, or school will help to organize counselors' thinking for potential interventions.

Reflective Questions

✓ Do most schools tolerate relational and social aggression among students and why?

✓ Do most administrators and teachers know how to define relational and social aggression?

✓ How can a counselor educate administrators and teachers on the potential harm of relational and social aggression?

Measuring Relational and Social Aggression

2

Mrs. Kennison is a fourth-grade teacher at Young Elementary School. During the first month of the school year, this teacher with five years of experience approaches the school counselor to discuss student dynamics in her classroom. Mrs. Kennison reports that most of her students refuse to participate in whole-class discussions or activities. She has tried to entice students in myriad ways to get them to participate more often. She has held class meetings, talked about the importance of participation and open discussion, and has given out free homework passes when students offer to give answers in class or come to the board to work out problems. The boys are more willing to take her up on these offers; however, Mrs. Kennison believes that overall, the incentives are not working consistently, and she is concerned that "nonparticipation" will become habit for most of the students in her class.

Mrs. Kennison informs the school counselor that some of the students appear quite anxious when she calls on them, and they often look to two of the class leaders (Sadie, age 11, and Marcia, age 10) before and after they answer questions. Mrs. Kennison has noticed that Sadie and Marcia have a "following" of other female and male students who want to hang around with them. When they are "permitted" to be around Sadie and Marcia, some of these students or followers are mean to others in the class or seem to act out of character. Sadie and Marcia have also been known to ignore other girls in the class, causing some tears among female students after recess or

Authors' Note: Some information in this chapter has been adapted from the work of the following authors: Crothers, L. M., Field, J. E., Kolbert, J. B., Bell, G. R., Blasik, J. L., Camic, L. A., Greisler, M. J., & Keener, D. (2007). Relational aggression in childhood and adolescence: Etiology, characteristics, diagnostic assessment, and treatment. *Counseling and Human Development, 39,* 1–24.

after lunch. Mrs. Kennison has talked with Sadie and Marcia about this privately; however, she still receives reports, sometimes through anonymous notes to her, that Sadie and Marcia are "mean." She has never directly observed this behavior by either girl.

The school counselor, Mr. Cummins, suggests that Mrs. Kennison give her students a brief questionnaire (see, for example, Appendix: Social Aggression Vignettes) to gather more information about the presence of relational and social aggression in her classroom. The students may not have reported on this specific type of bullying before because no one has asked them.

After completing the questionnaire, the teacher can examine the results and then pass the completed questionnaires to the school counselor. Based on the results, Mr. Cummins will then brainstorm ideas for classroom guidance lessons and small group counseling opportunities to improve classroom dynamics and social skills. Mrs. Kennison and Mr. Cummins collaborate and form a plan for how to proceed.

Teachers tend to be data-based decision makers, frequently measuring their students' progress on a daily or weekly basis. Often, educators use this information to determine whether pupils in their classrooms have mastered the academic material presented. If mastery has been achieved, the teacher feels comfortable moving ahead to tackle the next topic or theory. Conversely, if students have not sufficiently understood information or tested well on the material presented, teachers often return to the information and devise alternative ways of presenting the curriculum so that students have another opportunity to learn and demonstrate mastery.

Despite educators' comfort with measurement and evaluation of students' academic progress, teachers often feel reluctant to use assessment methods to investigate nonacademic problems, believing that such domains are best handled by the training and skills demonstrated by counselors and psychologists. However, as demonstrated in the scenario with Mrs. Kennison, nonacademic issues can interfere with classroom participation and student productivity—both of which are keys to academic success. Counselors need to remind teachers that they have all the skills necessary to compile, gather, and evaluate information not only regarding children's and adolescents' academic proficiency but also their behavior and social skills. In addition, teachers, along with counselors and psychologists, all provide different perspectives about children's behavioral and social functioning. Since bullying behavior, including relational and social aggression, is a significant problem in many schools in the United States, in addition to counselors and psychologists, teachers can be a valuable resource in engaging in this important first step in providing a solution.

Why should measurement of relational and social aggression be an important element of solving the problem of student bullying at school? First, it is necessary to recognize that bullying problems, including those of social and relational aggression, can undermine children's and adolescents' ability to learn. In order for children and adolescents to be able to concentrate on academic activities, they must have their basic needs met, including those of nutrition, sleep, acceptance, and safety (Maslow, 1943). When children or adolescents are neglected or rejected by peers at school, their feelings of psychological safety and well-being may be compromised. Consequently, in order to facilitate student learning, educators must begin by ensuring a safe learning environment, and measuring bullying problems in the classroom is a necessary step in this process. Only by measuring relational and social aggression can precise, timely, and effective prevention and intervention techniques be used to combat this common problem of childhood and adolescence.

Another compelling reason to measure relational and social aggression is to establish that it is a problem that educators and parents must take seriously. Without local data suggesting that children and adolescents are struggling with bullying, it may be easy to overlook these issues in light of the myriad of other difficulties facing students and teachers in our nation's schools. When educators provide evidence of the problem of bullying by tracking such information as incidence rates and negative outcomes of the behavior (both for perpetrators and victims), administrators or school board members may be more likely to see the problem as significant and respond accordingly with calls for increased services and programming. Similarly, parents who are presented with objective information regarding their child's or adolescent's role in bullying perhaps may respond with greater urgency in recognizing that intervention is necessary.

Despite the necessity of measurement, it is helpful to recognize, however, that diagnostic assessment of relational and social aggression, generally speaking, is far more difficult than assessment of other forms of aggression because of its covert characteristics (Merrell et al., 2006). While physical and verbal bullying include more easily identifiable behavior such as pushing, kicking and hitting, or name-calling and verbal harassment, relational and social aggression are often harder to detect because the behaviors are often subtle or happen away from the counselor's or teacher's supervision. In this chapter, several methods are presented that can be used to help educators measure relational and social aggression at school. Although the previous chapter focused on relational and social aggression among girls and adolescent females, it may be helpful for an educator to measure the incidences of relational and social aggression across males and females. Counselors and teachers can then determine if the subsequent interventions should be gender focused or be relevant for males and females. Each diagnostic technique has specific disadvantages; different assessment methods provide unique contributions to identifying, understanding, and treating relational and social aggression (see Table 2.1 for a summary of each technique).

Table 2.1   Strengths and Weaknesses of Measurement Techniques

Measurement Technique	Strengths	Weaknesses
Sociometric Techniques	• Helps counselors, psychologists, and teachers understand the dynamics of children's peer groups • Students offer a unique perspective about their peers • Useful when planning whole-class interventions	• Students may inaccurately report data to manipulate adults • Teacher and parent perspectives are not considered • Child- or adolescent-generated issues are not considered
Questionnaires and Surveys	• Information is comprehensive and easily gathered • Useful when planning whole-school interventions	• Teacher and parent perspectives are not considered • Child- or adolescent-generated issues are not considered
Teacher Rating Scales and Reports	• Teachers offer a unique perspective about their students	• Information may be biased • Teachers lack direct knowledge of what happens outside of school
Parent Rating Scales and Reports	• Children may be less afraid to report victimization to parents, thereby giving more accurate information	• Information may be biased • Parents lack direct knowledge of what happens at school
Student Self-Reports	• Provides firsthand information about perpetrators and contexts of victimization	• Students may inaccurately report data to manipulate adults • Perpetrators may underreport aggression

Measurement Technique	Strengths	Weaknesses
	• Offers an opportunity to measure children's or adolescents' overall psychological well-being	• Victims may underreport victimization
Interviews	• Yields a great amount of information about participants, contexts, specific behaviors, relationships, coping styles, and frequency of relational and social aggression • Children and adolescents can talk about issues that may not otherwise have been addressed	• Information may be more subjective and less verifiable than other methods • Students may inaccurately report data to manipulate adults
Focus Groups/Analyzing Language	• May provide more information because students build off others' ideas • Can be used as exercises in prevention or intervention	• Information may be more subjective and less verifiable than other methods
Observations	• Yields a great amount of information about participants, contexts, specific behaviors, and frequency of relational and social aggression	• May not offer a "true" picture because counselors and teachers cannot observe students in all settings, behavior may be hidden from adults, or the observer may not be able to monitor for a sufficient amount of time

Counselors and teachers may be understandably concerned regarding the time investment required to engage in assessment of relational and social aggression. Teachers may believe that measuring such behaviors among their students does not fall within the purview of teacher-assigned tasks. However, unquestionably, teachers have the most contact with students on a day-to-day basis and are able to identify the behavior patterns and practices that distract students from their school work or interrupt the establishment or maintenance of a safe learning environment in a classroom. In response to these types of concerns, this chapter will help counselors understand many different types of measurement techniques so that they can assist teachers with identifying the approach that best fits the needs of the classroom, school building, or educational system. For example, in order to conduct a quick examination of the scope of the problem of bullying in a small group of students or in a classroom, an educator could select one of the survey techniques presented later in the chapter. Conversely, for a more thorough analysis of the problem, school administrators may request a combination of assessment techniques, such as student, teacher, and parent reports in order to design a schoolwide program that adequately addresses all types of bullying behaviors.

> When time is an issue, educators can reproduce one of the measurement techniques designed for children and adolescents in this chapter (e.g., a survey) and simply have each student anonymously complete the form.

Before deciding to undertake a specific assessment approach, one question that counselors and teachers might have is, "What data is yielded after an assessment is conducted?" Assessment approaches can provide such information as who are the perpetrators and victims in incidents of relational and social aggression, are they primarily female or male, where do the behaviors occur (e.g., in the lunchroom, during art class, off school grounds), how is the victimization is carried out (e.g., through gossip, text messaging, social Web sites), and what are the consequences or results of the behavior for both initiators and recipients. When counselors, psychologists, and teachers obtain such information, they may be better equipped to design prevention and intervention approaches responsive to relational and social aggression. For example, if an educator found that most relational or social victimization occurred via text messaging on cellular (cell) telephones during the school day, such devices could be limited to before and after school use only to diminish the opportunity of disruption during academic time. Furthermore, a counselor or teacher could alert parents that this behavior was occurring among their children or adolescents and encourage monitoring of cell-phone use to diminish the opportunity for offending and victimization. Or if most relational and social aggression occurred during lunch, more personnel could be assigned to monitor the lunchroom and to proactively interact with the students.

What information can be provided when educators assess bullying behavior?

✓ Who are the perpetrators?

✓ Who are the victims?

✓ Where does the bullying occur?

✓ How is the victimization carried out?

✓ What happens after the behavior occurs?

Another query might be how often measurement of relational and social aggression occurs. The answer to this question varies depending upon the reason why the educator is gathering information regarding relational and social aggression. For example, if the purpose of measurement is to obtain a sense of the frequency or severity of the problem, the counselor or teacher could do so once or twice a schoolyear or before and after an intervention is in place. Similarly, if the educator is engaging in assessment techniques to identify the perpetrators or victims of the bullying, this could be done a few times each school year. Since the schedule and type of measurement selected depends upon the question the teacher or administrator wants to answer, he or she can determine which approach will best fit with the anticipated frequency of assessment. Several examples are included throughout this chapter in order to give educators flexibility in their choices.

Need to measure all kinds of bullying behavior? No problem. Simply add the characteristics of physical and verbal bullying to those of relational and social bullying described in Table 2.5 on page 50. Olweus (1993) provides a detailed description of all bullying behaviors in his book, *Bullying at School: What We Know and What We Can Do.*

So what if an educator wishes to assess all kinds of bullying behavior instead of simply focusing upon relational and social aggression? Interestingly, educators can assess for different types of bullying concurrently, either by combining the approaches provided throughout the chapter with measurements targeting physical and verbal bullying or by simply adding the characteristics of physical and verbal bullying to the descriptions of relational and social bullying contained in various assessment methods. Since this book is designed specifically to address issues of relational and social aggression, the assessment examples provided are specifically tailored to measure these types of bullying. Regardless of whether an educator is specifically targeting relational and social aggression or focused upon reducing bullying behavior in general—including measurement in a comprehensive approach to prevent or intervene in childhood bullying problems—it is prudent and ethical to assess these examples since the information obtained can precisely and comprehensively inform prevention and intervention efforts.

SOCIOMETRIC PROCEDURES

One of the most common forms of diagnostic assessment is sociometric measurement, which includes peer nomination, peer rating, and peer ranking (Merrell et al., 2006). These techniques are often used when educators are interested in learning about the dynamics of children's peer groups. In sociometric assessment methods, counselors or teachers can ask children to report about their peers' social behaviors such as which children or adolescents in the classroom or at school fit a certain social profile (peer nomination), have specified behavioral characteristics (peer rating), or can be ranked from most to least on a set of behaviors (peer ranking). Figure 2.1 provides an example of how to use a sociometric technique at your school.

Figure 2.1   Sociometric Technique

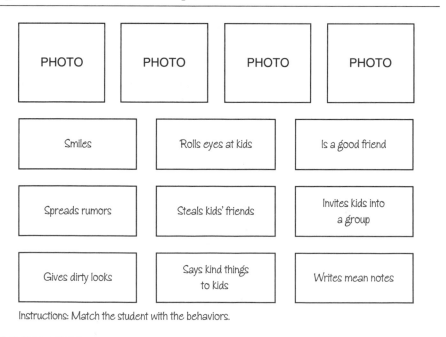

Instructions: Match the student with the behaviors.

The reason such methods are used is because children often offer a unique perspective about their peers, unlike that of teachers or parents. Students have almost complete access to other youngsters in the classroom and can observe behaviors that their peers may hide from adults. Although counselors and teachers often have a good sense of children's and adolescents' peer acceptance, it can be argued that students provide the most accurate information about their own and others' peer status (Mayeux, Underwood, & Risser, 2007). Sociometric procedures are useful when planning whole-class interventions since every child or adolescent in the classroom is considered in the measurement process. Again, if females are primarily highlighted as perpetrators of relational and social aggression, the teacher and counselor will need to come up with creative strategies (e.g., group counseling, workshops for girls) to focus on females.

Peer Nomination

In peer nomination, students are asked to name other children or adolescents from class rosters who behave in relationally or socially aggressive ways. A helpful method of obtaining information concerning the participants in relational victimization, particularly for young children, is through a picture sociometric method in which students are provided with a photograph of each of their classmates and asked to separate the photographs into two piles—those who relationally and socially bully others and those who do not. Children then can be asked to do the same for children who are relationally and socially bullied and those who are not (see Figure 2.2; Bowers, Smith, & Binney, 1994: Crothers & Levinson, 2004).

Figure 2.2   Peer Nomination

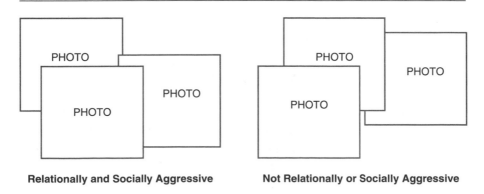

Relationally and Socially Aggressive   **Not Relationally or Socially Aggressive**

This approach is done individually with each student to protect his or her privacy during the assessment. Furthermore, although it may be a time-consuming process, it may yield excellent insight into peer dynamics that are undetected by educators.

Peer Rating

Peer rating methods include such techniques as asking students to rate peers' relationally or socially aggressive behaviors using a Likert scale (e.g., 1 = never, 2 = occasionally, 3 = sometimes, 4 = often, 5 = always). An example of this method is asking children to indicate the number of times they saw a particular student behave relationally aggressively during the previous week (Coyne et al., 2006). Additionally, children and adolescents can be asked to rate the degree of harm of various aggressive behaviors, giving educators information regarding students' perceptions of how severe each behavior is to them.

Peer Ranking

In the peer-ranking method, counselors can create a definition of relationally and socially aggressive behaviors (see Table 2.5 on page 50 for behavioral descriptors) and ask students to rank their peers from most to least relationally or socially aggressive. In the case of young children, educators can ask children to place peers' photographs in a hierarchy, while for older children or adolescents, counselors, may have students rank students from a classroom roster of names. Conversely, educators can have students rank their peers from most to least on victim characteristics. Prior to an assessment with older students, counselors and/or educators must remind participants that their answers are anonymous and that peers should not pressure other peers to tell them what they wrote on the peer-ranking instrument.

QUESTIONNAIRES AND SURVEYS

Educators and counselors can also use questionnaires or surveys to assess bullying in their classrooms or school. Such methods are useful when planning whole-school interventions because a large amount of information is yielded in a relatively short time. In Figures 2.3 and 2.4, the Adolescent Social Behavior Scale—Perpetrator and Victim forms are presented for educators to use. Developed by the authors, both of these forms should be given to each adolescent in the classroom or the school in order to gather anonymous data about the incidence of relationally and socially

Figure 2.3 Adolescent Social Behavior Victim Scale

Directions: Please put a check next to the appropriate frequency in which you engage in each of the following behaviors.

Behavior	Never 5	Sometimes 4	Occasionally 3	Frequently 2	Always 1
1. When a friend/classmate/sibling is angry with me, I am often the last to know. He or she will talk with others first.					
2. When a friend/classmate/sibling is frustrated or irritated with me, he or she will stop talking to me.					
3. Others talk to me in an honest, straightforward manner when we are having an interpersonal problem.					
4. When a friend/classmate/sibling doesn't like my personality, he or she derives a certain degree of pleasure when someone else listens to and agrees with his/her assessment of my personality.					
5. My friends/classmates/siblings tell rumors at school or home.					
6. My friends/classmates/siblings honor my need for secrets or confidentiality.					
7. A friend may tell my secrets to others just to have a good story to tell.					
8. My friends/classmates/siblings confront me in public to achieve maximum damage.					
9. People who are close to me criticize me.					
10. My friends respect my opinions, even when they are quite different from their own.					
11. My friends intentionally exclude me from activities to make a point with me.					
12. A rival has attempted to "steal" one of my friends.					
13. When a friend is angry with me, he or she has threatened to end the relationship in hopes that I will comply with his or her wishes.					
14. My friends believe that working through conflicts makes our friendship stronger.					

Figure 2.4 Adolescent Social Behavior Perpetrator Scale

Directions: Please put a check next to the appropriate frequency in which you engage in each of the following behaviors.

Behavior	Never	Sometimes	Occasionally	Frequently	Always
	5	4	3	2	1
1. When I am angry with someone, that person is often the last person to know. I will talk to others first.					
2. When I am frustrated with my friend/classmate/sibling, I give that person the silent treatment.					
3. I deal with interpersonal conflict in an honest, straightforward manner.					
4. When I do not like someone's personality, I derive a certain degree of pleasure when a friend listens to and agrees to my assessment of the person's personality.					
5. I contribute to the rumor mill at school/work or with my friends and family.					
6. I honor my friends' needs for secrets and confidentiality.					
7. I break a friend's confidentiality to have a good story to tell					
8. I confront people in public to achieve maximum damage.					
9. I criticize people who are close to me.					
10. I respect my friends' opinions, even when they are quite different from my own.					
11. I intentionally exclude friends from activities to make a point with them.					
12. I have attempted to "steal" a rival's friend.					
13. When I am angry with a friend, I have threatened to sever the relationship in hopes that the person will comply with my wishes.					
14. Working through conflicts with friends makes our friendship stronger.					

aggressive behaviors. Results can be compiled and aggregated so that educators may understand how often students perceive perpetration or victimization by such behaviors.

Another example is the Social Behavior Questionnaire located in Figure 2.5 (pages 40–41) in which there are 12 vignettes that describe social interactions between same-sex peers (Galen & Underwood, 1997).

TEACHER RATING SCALES AND REPORTS

Another common form of assessment consists of teacher ratings of relational and social aggression. In completing these scales, teachers are asked to nominate students who are perceived to be the most frequent perpetrators or victims of relational and social aggression (see Figure 2.6 on page 42 for an example of a teacher rating scale). Although this method can yield reliable data, there is the potential for some bias depending upon the way in which teachers perceive actions from different students. These issues, however, can be balanced with more direct and less subjective means of measuring relational aggression, such as observations by other school personnel (Merrell et al., 2006). Teachers can also provide informal interview reports about students' relationally and socially aggressive behavior.

While some researchers (Lagerspetz, Björkqvist, Berts, & King, 1982; Olweus, 1993) have suggested teacher nominations are accurate, others believe that teachers may grossly underestimate the amount of peer aggression that actually takes place at school (Smith & Sharp, 1994). When utilizing such ratings, educators must consider the possibility of teacher bias toward the student and differences in perception related to the child's age (Pellegrini & Bartini, 2000). Teachers' ratings are the result of their own experiences with students in specific settings, and inaccurate information may result if teachers observe students in a limited number of settings. Therefore, it is better when teachers spend long periods of time observing children and adolescents in a variety of settings and maintain their objectivity through checking their observations with others' experiences with the same children and adolescents (Pellegrini & Bartini, 2000).

PARENT REPORTS

Parents can be a valuable source of information about their children's social status among peers. Often, children and adolescents confess the problems they are having with other students in their classroom to their parents after being questioned about seeming sad or worried at home.

40

Figure 2.5 Social Behavior Questionnaire

Directions: Imagine that these situations happen to you and put a checkmark in the appropriate box.

	Not at All	Rarely/ A Little	Sometimes/ Somewhat	Frequently/ Extremely	Very Much
During class, a girl passes you a note that says: "No one wants to be your friend."					
How hurt would you be if this happened to you?					
How often does something like this happen in the group of people you hang around with?					
Four girls in your grade are talking about a movie they have just seen when you walk up to the group. The group sees you, stops talking, and turns away from you with their noses turned upward.					
How hurt would you be if this happened to you?					
How often does something like this happen in the group of people you hang around with?					
You hear two girls talking, and they don't see you. One girl says, "I heard that she's going to the party with Alex—but *I* wanted to go with him. Let's tell everyone that she did something awful—then maybe he'll go with me instead." Then they see you and say, "Be quiet! Here she is now."					
How hurt would you be if this happened to you?					
How often does something like this happen in the group of people you hang around with?					

	Not at All	Rarely/ A Little	Sometimes/ Somewhat	Frequently/ Extremely	Very Much
Your teacher says that he or she will be assigning partners for a class project and tells you and another girl that you will be working together. The other girl looks at you, says, "*Her?*" then rolls her eyes and makes a face.					
How hurt would you be if this happened to you?					
How often does something like this happen in the group of people you hang around with?					
You are playing with a hand-held video game when a girl comes over to you, stands with her arms crossed and says, "I think your game is over now," and then glares at you.					
How hurt would you be if this happened to you?					
How often does something like this happen in the group of people you hang around with?					
During lunch, a group of girls are talking about the big party this Saturday. When you ask them if you're invited, they say, "You? I don't *think* so." Then they start laughing and walk away.					
How hurt would you be if this happened to you?					
How often does something like this happen in the group of people you hang around with?					

SOURCE: Copyright © 1997 by the American Psychological Association. B. R. Galen & M. K. Underwood (1997). A developmental investigation of social aggression among children. *Developmental Psychology, 33,* p. 600.. Reprinted with permission of the American Psychological Association. No further reproduction or distribution is permitted without written permission from the American Psychological Association.

Figure 2.6 Children's Social Behavior Scale—Teacher Form

Behavior	1 = This is never true of this child.	2 = This is occasionally true of this child.	3 = This is sometimes true of this child.	4 = This is often true of this child.	5 = This is always true of this child.
When this child is mad at a peer, she or he gets even by excluding the peer from his or her clique or peer group.					
This child spreads rumors or gossips about some peers.					
When angry at a peer, this child tries to get other children to stop playing with the peer or to stop liking the peer.					
This child tries to get others to dislike certain peers by telling lies about the peers to others.					
When mad at a peer, this child ignores the peer or stops talking to the peer.					
This child threatens to stop being a peer's friend in order to hurt the peer or to get what she or he wants from the peer.					
This child tries to exclude certain peers from peer-group activities.					
This child tries to dominate or bully peers.					

SOURCE: Adapted to show only the relationally aggressive items. From N. R. Crick (1996). The role of overt aggression, relational aggression, and pro-social behavior in the prediction of children's future social adjustment. *Child Development, 67,* p. 2321.

Alternately, other parents may question or inform a parent when his or her child or adolescent is socially and relationally victimizing peers at school. As is the case with teachers, though, parents may have a one-sided perspective of the problem and may not ever have the opportunity to directly witness the behavior their child or adolescent is perpetrating or experiencing. Because of this, it may be helpful to pair parent reports with peer or teacher reports or observations. In Figures 2.7 and 2.8 on pages 44–45, examples are provided of parent-report instruments that may be used with children or adolescents. Developed by the authors, both of these forms should be given to each parent in order to obtain information about the child's or adolescent's behavior.

Counselors or teachers can also interview parents either in person, over the telephone, or through e-mail about their child's behavior. While parents of children or adolescents who are bullying their peers may be reluctant to acknowledge a problem, educators can pose factual, non-blaming questions to parents about their youngster's behavior. Similarly, when communicating with parents of students who are being victimized, educators should convey empathy while avoiding blaming and recriminations regarding other children or adolescents, particularly before all of the facts have been gathered.

STUDENT SELF-REPORTS

Another valuable assessment method is self-reporting by students. This technique provides useful information because it not only offers counselors or teachers firsthand information about perpetrators of relational and social aggression and where such behavior occurs but also presents opportunities for informal evaluation of a child's or adolescent's overall psychological well-being. In Table 2.2 and 2.3 on pages 46–47, examples are provided of self-report instruments that may be used with adolescents.

In completing self-report measures, students may be asked to respond to questions about specific behaviors, as in the case of the previous examples, or may include hypothetical situations to which children or adolescents are to react. In one study, researchers presented hypothetical situations to aggressive students and measured their reactions. The scenarios depicted a positive friendship trait that was not present in the character's friendship and a negative quality that was a part of the character's relationship. The participant was asked to rate his or her desire to remain friends with the person exhibiting the negative personality trait described in the story (Crick & Grotpeter, 1996). In another example, students were

Figure 2.7 Parent Social Behavior Victim Scale

Directions: Please put a check next to the appropriate frequency in which you engage in each of the following behaviors.

Behavior	Never 5	Sometimes 4	Occasionally 3	Frequently 2	Always 1
1. When a friend, classmate, or sibling is angry with my child or adolescent, he or she is often the last to know. My child or adolescent's friends, classmates, or sibling will talk with others first.					
2. When a friend, classmate, or sibling is frustrated or irritated with my child or adolescent, he or she will stop talking to him or her.					
3. Others talk to my child or adolescent in an honest, straightforward manner when having an interpersonal problem.					
4. When a friend, classmate, or sibling doesn't like my child's or adolescent's personality, friends, classmates, or siblings derive a certain degree of pleasure when someone else listens to and agrees with his or her assessment of my child's or adolescent's personality.					
5. My child's or adolescent's friends, classmates, or siblings tell rumors about my child or adolescent at school or home.					
6. My child's or adolescent's friends, classmates, or siblings honor my child's or adolescent's need for secrets or confidentiality.					
7. My child's or adolescent's friend may tell his or her secrets to others just to have a good story to tell.					
8. Friends, classmates, or siblings confront my child or adolescent in public to achieve maximum damage.					
9. People who are close to my child or adolescent criticize him or her.					
10. My child's or adolescent's friends respect his or her opinions even when they are quite different from their own.					
11. My child's or adolescent's friends intentionally exclude him or her from activities to make a point.					
12. A rival has attempted to "steal" one of my child's or adolescent's friends.					
13. When a friend is angry with my child or adolescent, he or she has threatened to end the relationship in hopes that my child or adolescent will comply with his or her wishes.					
14. My child's or adolescent's friends believe that working through conflicts makes their friendship stronger.					

Figure 2.8 Parent Social Behavior Perpetrator Scale

Directions: Please put a check next to the appropriate frequency in which your child or adolescent engages in each of the following behaviors.

Behavior	Never	Sometimes	Occasionally	Frequently	Always
	5	4	3	2	1
1. When my child or adolescent is angry with someone, that person is often the last person to know. My child or adolescent talks to others first.					
2. When my child or adolescent is frustrated with his or her friend, classmate, or sibling, my child or adolescent gives that person the silent treatment.					
3. My child or adolescent deals with interpersonal conflict in an honest, straightforward manner.					
4. When my child or adolescent does not like someone's personality, my child or adolescent derives a certain degree of pleasure when a friend listens to and agrees with his or her assessment of the person's personality.					
5. My child or adolescent contributes to the rumor mill at school or work or with friends and family.					
6. My child or adolescent honors friends' need for secrets of confidentiality.					
7. My child or adolescent breaks a friend's confidentiality to have a good story to tell					
8. My child or adolescent confronts people in public to achieve maximum damage.					
9. My child or adolescent criticizes people who are close to him or her.					
10. My child or adolescent respects friends' opinions even when they are quite different from his or her own.					
11. My child or adolescent intentionally exclude friends from activities to make a point with them.					
12. My child or adolescent has attempted to "steal" a rival's friend.					
13. When angry with a friend, my child or adolescent has threatened to sever the relationship in hopes that the person will comply with his or her wishes.					
14. My child or adolescent believes that working through conflicts with friends makes the friendship stronger.					

45

Table 2.2   Revised Peer Experiences Questionnaire—Victim Version

	Never	Once or Twice	A Few Times	About Once a Week	A Few Times a Week
A teen left me out of what he or she was doing.					
A teen left me out of an activity or conversation that I really wanted to be included in.					
A teen did not invite me to a party or other social event though he or she knew I wanted to go.					
A teen I wanted to be with would not sit near me at lunch or in class.					
A teen gave me the silent treatment (did not to talk to me on purpose).					

SOURCE: M. J. Prinstein, J. Boergers, & E. M. Vernberg (2001). *Revised Peer Experiences Questionnaire—Victim Version* in Overt and relational aggression in adolescents: Social-psychological adjustment of aggressors and victims. *Journal of Clinical Child Psychology, 30,* p. 483.

given social stories containing interpersonal conflict scenarios common to adolescent and choices for ways to react. The students were then asked for their response (Pakaslahti & Keltikangas-Järvinen, 2000). Educators can use such methods to gain insight into students' social problem-solving skills and tendencies for behavioral responses.

When school counselors, school psychologists, or teachers choose to use student self-report methods to assess for relational and social aggression, it is important to recognize that self-reports of aggression usually underestimate actual behavior because the perpetrators, in the interest of maintaining social desirability, often are reluctant to identify themselves (Pellegrini & Bartini, 2000). Consequently, educators should keep in mind that information given by suspected relationally or socially aggressive students might be only part of the real truth.

Table 2.3   Revised Peer Experiences Questionnaire—Aggressor Version

	Never	Once or Twice	A Few Times	About Once a Week	A Few Times a Week
I left a teen out of what I was doing.					
I left a teen out of an activity or conversation that he or she really wanted to be included in.					
I did not invite a teen to a party or other social event though I knew he or she wanted to go.					
I would not sit near a teen that wanted to be with me at lunch or in class.					
I gave a teen the silent treatment (did not to talk to him or her on purpose).					

SOURCE: M. J. Prinstein, J. Boergers, & E. M. Vernberg (2001). *Revised Peer Experiences Questionnaire—Aggressor Version* in Overt and relational aggression in adolescents: Social-psychological adjustment of aggressors and victims. *Journal of Clinical Child Psychology, 30,* p. 483.

INTERVIEW STRATEGIES

Interviews can be used by counselors and teachers to record the frequency of relational and social aggression, the effect of such bullying on students, and the impact of bullying interventions should they already be in place. Interviewing the victim can yield specific information about location, perceptions of the relationships with the aggressors, and means of coping, both behaviorally and emotionally (Casey-Cannon, Hayward, & Gowen, 2001). Moreover, in an interview, school children have an opportunity to speak about issues regarding relational and social aggression that may not be addressed in more structured assessment measures (Glover, Gough, Johnson, & Cartwright, 2000).

Field, Crothers, & Kolbert (2006) have developed a number of useful prompts that could be used by educators in an unstructured interview assessing relational and social aggression, such as, "When my close friends are angry with me . . . ," "I often think . . . ," "When I have a disagreement with my friends . . . ," "My parents expect me to . . . ," "When I have a fight with my friends, I deal with it by . . . ," and "When I disagree with someone who is equal to me in power or popularity, I will. . . ." The respondents, therefore, are responsible for constructing their own answers, which leaves room for the possibility of any number of answers. An example of an interview is provided in Table 2.4.

When conducting interviews, educators should recognize that interviews might be subjective and vulnerable to bias because of the interviewers' preconceptions or viewpoints (Crothers & Levinson, 2004). Consequently, it is advisable to pair interviews with sociometric methods, teacher, or self-report measures or to use interviewing as a part of preventing or intervening in instances of bullying.

FOCUS GROUPS

Another means of gathering information regarding relational aggression is to conduct group interviews or focus groups. This methodology has a synergistic effect in which participants build upon each other's responses, developing a richness and complexity of ideas through sharing and collaborating. Counselors can begin by presenting a vignette in which a child or adolescent is being relationally or socially victimized by peers, such as a girl returning to school after being absent for one day only to find that her friendship group now is ignoring her and spreading unkind rumors about her (Owens, Slee, & Shute, 2000). Counselors can expand their discussions by inquiring about similar kinds of scenarios in their school, the implications of such behavior, and typical reactions by students at the school. Not only can such an approach be used to gather information about social and relational aggression, but also the approach can be used as an intervention to encourage empathy among students as well as to emphasize the consequences of engaging in such behavior.

OBSERVATIONS

Counselors and teachers may also choose to use observational techniques to obtain information about relational and social aggression in their classroom or school. Observations can take two forms—structured and unstructured.

Table 2.4   Interview

1. When my close friends are angry with me, I often think _____.

2. When my close friends are angry with me, I often feel _____.

3. When my close friends are angry with someone, they expect me to____.

4. When I get angry at a boy, I will _____.

5. When I get angry at a girl, I will _____.

6. When I have a disagreement with my friends, my parents expect me to _____.

7. When I have a disagreement with my friends at school, my teachers expect me to _____.

8. When I have a fight with my friends, I deal with it by_____.

9. When I believe I am being treated unfairly, I _____.

10. When I disagree with a popular girl, I will _____.

11. When I disagree with someone who is equal to me in power (equal level of popularity), I will _____.

12. When people get angry with me, I have a right to _____.

13. In order to deal with my angry feelings toward my friends, I will _____.

14. In order for me to be open, honest, and straightforward with my angry feelings, I need _____.

15. When I am angry with others, sometimes I fear _____.

16. If I have an opinion that is different from my friends, I will _____.

SOURCE: Field, J. E., Crothers, L. M., & Kolbert, J. B. (2006). Fragile friendships: Exploring the use and effects of indirect aggression among adolescent girls. *Journal of School Counseling*, 4, Retrieved October 24, 2006 from http://www.jsc.montana.edu/articles/v4n5.pdf. Reprinted by permission of the publisher.

A structured observation involves gathering quantitative information such as frequency, duration, and symptoms of relational and social aggression. An unstructured observation involves gathering information during peak relational and social aggression periods such as recess. Observations potentially yield much information about participants, settings, forms, and frequency of these types of bullying. Observational measures usually do not correlate well over time, however, perhaps because of limited observation samples and children's or adolescents' behavior

Table 2.5   Observation Form

Directions: Use a ✓ to represent behaviors by the target student and the comparison peer.

Behavior	Target Student	Comparison Peer
Dirty looks *		
Exclusion from a group ***		
Eye-rolling *		
Ignoring ***		
Isolating ****		
Gossiping ***		
Mean verbal remarks ***		
Speaking to someone in a cold or hostile tone ***		
Spreading rumors ***		
Staring ***		
Stealing friends or boyfriends ****		
Writing nasty notes **		

SOURCE: Relationally and Socially Aggressive Behaviors were taken from Archer & Coyne (2005)*, Coyne, Archer, & Eslea (2006)**, Remillard & Lamb (2005)***, and Xie, Swift, Cairns, & Cairns (2002)****.

changing to suit the context. These weaknesses can be minimized by sampling behavior in multiple settings over long periods of time (Pellegrini & Bartini, 2000).

Direct observation methods also may not measure the true prevalence and magnitude of bullying behavior because relational and social aggression often is covert (Colvin, Tobin, Beard, Hagan, & Sprague, 1998; Olweus, 1993). Educators' observations reflect a public (normative) perspective and cannot be conducted in some school settings, such as restrooms or locker rooms, where bullying tends to occur. Other obstacles include the possibility that relational bullies simply may cease to engage in aggressive behavior when they are aware that they are being observed (Cole, Cornell, & Sheras, 2006). As mentioned earlier in the chapter, relational and social aggression can be a relatively difficult phenomenon to observe because it often is not seen as physical aggression is (Young, Boye, & Nelson, 2006).

ETHICAL CONSIDERATIONS IN ASSESSMENT

When engaging in any of the assessment methods described in this chapter, counselors should be conscious of ethical considerations such as confidentiality, informed consent, and potential risks involved with subjective assessment (i.e., one student indentifying problematic behaviors demonstrated by a peer). In measuring relational and social aggression and children's social status among peers, the confidentially of the students must be strictly maintained given the potential for increased victimization by peers. Prior to using an assessment tool in a classroom, teachers and/or counselors should talk directly with the students about the assessment.

Specific talking points may include the following:

- Concern about the way in which students are relating to one another or that students are having difficulty getting along with one another
- Awareness that lack of student comfort or sense of belonging in a class distracts students from what is being taught, which interferes with learning
- Expectations for student behavior, including following school rules, showing respect for other students in the class, demonstrating honesty, and an effort to get along with each another
- Results of the instrument will be used to make decisions for how to improve the class environment for all students
- Students should not put their names on the instrument and should not share their answers with other people in the class
- Students should be honest with their responses and know that their peers will not know what they wrote on their instrument
- Students should not ask each other what they wrote as the information is confidential

Of course teachers cannot ensure that students will not ask one another about the instrument; however, teachers can talk with the class as a whole about their expectations if they learn that students are attempting to find out what students have written or using the information as leverage against other students. Some research has examined the effect of assessing children's social status and behaviors with children reporting that they were not hurt or upset by sociometric techniques, did not feel that their peers treated them differently after testing, and understood their rights in participating in such assessment methods (Mayeux et al., 2007). Additionally, the potential ethical quandary in asking children to identify peers' relational aggression in a sociometric technique can be relieved by requesting that youngsters report on pro-social behavior in their classmates as well.

If educators are concerned about whether their impressions of students are biased and thus affecting the accuracy of the information gathered through measurement approaches, it is recommended that teachers compare their impressions with those of other teachers or staff members who observe students in different classrooms or contexts. Additionally, teacher observations can be supplemented with the use of journals in which children and adolescents can record behavior on standardized forms at predetermined intervals, thereby offering a private perspective of bullying (Pellegrini, 1996). The reliability and validity of such diaries is increased when participants record their behavior using specific vocabulary or categories at specific times (Pellegrini & Bartini, 2000).

> Tip: Make sure parents of children or adolescents directly involved in assessment of relational and social aggression give consent before proceeding with any measurement techniques.

It is important that the parents of the children or adolescents involved in assessment of relational and social aggression sign consent forms allowing their child or adolescent to participate and that children or adolescents sign assent forms signifying their willingness to participate. Counselors and teachers should respect the wishes of parents who do not wish for their children to participate in such measurement, although educators should also recognize that less-than-complete-classroom participation might affect the accuracy of the assessments (Merrell et al., 2006).

CONCLUSION

Measurement of behaviors, such as relational and social aggression, can be as straightforward as measuring academic achievement in children and adolescents. With careful planning, educators can select from several different assessment techniques and obtain rich, accurate information about types of bullying that may be occurring in the classroom or at school. In this chapter, there are examples of most of the measurement approaches that can be used to assess relational and social aggression in children and adolescents, and it is recommended that two or more assessment techniques be employed in order to provide a comprehensive account of bullying behavior. Educators are encouraged to consider the ethical guidelines that pertain to measuring students' behavior and to consult with support staff such as counselors, administrators, or psychologists if they have questions related to this topic. Finally, accurate measurement can lead to more effective intervention efforts. In Chapter 3, counselors will be presented with various forms of intervention.

Reflective Questions

✓ How can the perception of not having enough time to conduct assessment of relational and social behaviors in children and adolescents undermine educators' work in effectively addressing this problem?

✓ Why is combining assessment approaches from different stakeholders (e.g., teachers, parents, students) recommended instead of using only one technique?

✓ As you continue to the next chapter, think about how information gathered from assessing relationally and socially aggressive behaviors can be used in an intervention plan.

School-Based
Interventions

3

Maya Jones, her mother, and her grandmother sit together outside of the school counselor's office. All have stern faces and don't speak to one another while they wait. The purpose of the meeting is to discuss Maya's recent decision to drop her honors courses for the following academic year. She has decided that she does not want to attend college. Maya is currently a junior, has earned straight A's throughout most of her high school career, and would be the first in her family to attend a university. Miss Waki, school counselor, is aware of Maya's schedule-change request and is hoping that the meeting will shed light on why Maya has changed her mind. As the meeting begins, Mrs. Jones, Maya's mother, explains that Maya has changed so much over the last year that she "barely recognizes" her daughter. Maya's grandmother states that Maya doesn't study as much as she used to, is forced to attend church now, is not on the track team for the first time since middle school, and does not hang out with her friends as "the younger folk" typically do. Maya does not make eye contact with anyone as her eyes fill with tears. Miss Waki considers all of the possible explanations for this change. Maya had come to see her at the beginning of the school year. She was distraught about losing two of her closest friends. Maya explained that the trouble began when she began dating a popular football player, won two academic achievement awards at an assembly, and was elected to be student council vice-president. With a caseload of 600 students, Miss Waki had not followed up with Maya after their two counseling sessions. How can she help Maya now?

Intervention refers to individual, group, or systematic efforts to reduce, eliminate, or alleviate a particular problem or set of problems. After conducting an assessment or assessments to measure the prevalence of relational and social aggression among students, counselors must then decide how to intervene in an effective, developmentally and systemically appropriate manner. Addressing relational and social aggression at school, as with bullying in general, may fall into three categories: primary, secondary, and tertiary intervention. Primary prevention programs occur in a school environment and are generally educational in nature. The focus is on the development of social and cognitive skills through educational programming to reduce relationally and socially aggressive behaviors. In this type of programming, normal developmental skills of children and adolescents are highlighted. For example, counselors can conduct classroom guidance lessons on communication skills, problem solving, perspective taking, assertiveness, and conflict resolution. Classroom teachers or administrators can then reinforce students who practice or approximate behaviors that are consistent with healthy skills in these areas.

Secondary intervention programs include larger scale, school-based, anti-violence curricula to address children's and adolescents' social competence through the development of empathy and perspective-taking, social problem solving, assertiveness, emotion regulation, and anger-management skills. Examples of this type of intervention may include a gradewide assembly that educates students on different forms of bullying (e.g., physical aggression, relational and social aggression, cyberbullying), ways to manage bullies, and the school's policies regarding all types of bullying at school. The primary difference between primary and secondary interventions is the explicit and comprehensive focus on identifying and coping with undesirable behavior at the broad systems level rather than focusing on prevention at the classroom level. These approaches are similar in their focus on pro-social problem-solving skills that accompany typical development.

Finally, tertiary prevention programs provide intervention to those who are at risk or already involved in relationally aggressive behaviors or conflicts. This may include victims and perpetrators with individual interventions tailored to address new skill development for the child or adolescent. For example, a female student who consistently instigates conflict with her peers may participate in an individual counseling intervention focused on understanding the viewpoint of others (e.g., perspective taking), the role of empathy in governing behaviors, and identifying what thoughts guide her relational or socially aggressive behaviors.

Primary: Focus is prevention. Teach social skills to reduce the likelihood of bullying. Mostly used at the classroom or grade level.

Secondary: Focus is prevention and intervention. Large scale, comprehensive (i.e., schoolwide) efforts with the goal of reducing incidents of relational and social aggression and preventing future use of this type of bullying (e.g., school assemblies, teacher trainings, peer educator/helper programs).

Tertiary: Focus is on intervention. Individual and/or group counseling aimed at "at risk individuals or small groups of students who are actively involved in relational and social aggression or who may be at risk for involvement in relational or social aggression (e.g., perpetrators or victims).

FACTORS IN SELECTING INTERVENTIONS

School administrators, teachers, counselors, and psychologists may be eager to help students and their parents address issues related to relational and social aggression. The type of intervention should be based on the needs of students in a particular school, grade, or class, which can be measured through the use of various assessment tools (see Chapter 2). Furthermore, school personnel also need to be open to examining the school context and how practices within the system may actually permit or support relational or social aggression. It is often the culture of a school that has the most influence over maintaining or eliminating relational or social aggression. For example, schools that have the most detailed and comprehensive anti-bullying policies (e.g., bullying defined as overt verbal and physical bullying) tend to be those with the *highest* incidence of relational aggression among their students (Woods & Wolke, 2003). Many schools construct anti-bullying policies that do not include language regarding social forms of bullying behavior. Therefore, if students are aware of the consequences for physical bullying, they may instead resort to social forms of bullying that are more difficult to detect by authority figures. Furthermore, if these students are detected, and a clear policy regarding relational and social is missing, applying consequences for these behaviors is less clear.

If students have not been educated on the various forms of bullying, they may not recognize that what they are doing (e.g., spreading rumors, social isolations) as bullying behavior. Students may report "my friends are my choice; I do not have to like, play, call, socialize, or befriend anyone I don't want to." While freedom to select and nurture a friendship is an individual choice, creating a school climate where certain students are isolated, undermined, or targeted is not. Students require explicit instruction on how to be a good citizen of the school rather than to agree (implicitly or explicitly) to a friendship. Similarly, in schools where teachers are less aware of the negative social and emotional outcomes of relational aggression, including impact on the learning environment, there tends to be a limited focus on acknowledging relational and socially aggressive behaviors, let alone intervening in a systemic manner.

Teacher perceptions can be a key factor in how and when acts of relational or social aggression trigger the need for intervention. Bauman and Del Rio (2006) surveyed a group of preservice teachers and found that they rated relational aggression as less serious than physical or verbal bullying, reported less empathy for victims of relational aggression, and indicated that they were less likely to intervene. There are several potential explanations for why teachers choose not to intervene. First, teachers must be aware of what relational and social aggression is and what it looks like in order to spot these behaviors and label them appropriately. Counselors can be instrumental in helping teachers and administrators understand these forms of bullying through staff development opportunities and consultation with individual teachers. If a school does not have a clear policy that identifies social forms of bullying as behavior that is against school rules, educators may not believe that they have grounds for disciplining students who engage in social and relational aggression.

Teachers may also be guilty of categorizing particular students, just as children and adolescents often due, and may fail to act to protect a child that they too deem socially inept or annoying. If students report, "not even the teachers like Hannah," this is evidence that the teachers themselves may be unconsciously or consciously condoning the use of relational and social aggression or participating in it. Victims of this type of bullying may possess fewer social skills or may be socially awkward while perpetrators are often able to use their high levels of social intelligence to demean or manipulate others while simultaneously using their popularity to win the favor of their peers *and* teachers (Andreou, 2006; Bauman & Del Rio, 2006; Crothers et al., 2007). Regardless of teacher intention, the impact of failing to act must be explicitly understood by the teaching faculty. The salient issue is that relational and social aggression, just like physical aggression, can interfere with a student's ability to feel safe at school and thus interferes with their ability to feel connected to others in the school climate, focus on academic content, or thrive in the learning environment. It is the obligation of the school system to provide adequate training to faculty and staff so that the needs of children and adolescents are addressed.

Roecker-Phelps (2001) found that both boys and girls are equally likely to be the recipients of relational aggression; however, girls are more likely to respond negatively to social and relational forms of aggression (Crick, Bigbee, & Howes, 1996; Galen & Underwood, 1997; Paquette & Underwood, 1999). Roecker-Phelps (2001) hypothesizes that because girls use more subtle forms of coping such as ruminating, talking to parents and peers, and experiencing sadness and internal distress rather than the externalized style most often exhibited by boys, girls' distress is more likely to go unnoticed, and they remain underserved by educators' intervention efforts

(Yoon, Barton, & Taiariol, 2004). While primary and secondary forms of intervention may focus on boys and girls alike in helping them understand what relational and social aggression is, as well as alternatives to these bullying behaviors, tertiary interventions with females must highlight the way in which gender socialization of girls may actually enhance the consequences for victims or encourage the use of these behaviors by female perpetrators. Focusing on gender-specific aspects of relational and social aggression will render the intervention more effective and meaningful for the participants.

Educators must embrace the idea that when relational and social aggression is not addressed by individuals in authority, there is a negative effect on students' ability to engage in and benefit from the educational environment. That is, distracted by their discomfort, this group is less available to participate in classroom activities and assignments. Furthermore, these youth are less ready to benefit from the positive social context in schools, as they are often focused on vigilantly monitoring their social circles for signs of change or fluctuations and managing their negative feelings (e.g., sadness, anxiety) stemming from being victimized.

What happens when social and relational aggression is not addressed?

✓ Students are distracted by their emotional discomfort.

✓ Students are less available to participate in classroom activities.

✓ Students are cut off from friendships or peer support.

✓ Students are less ready to benefit from the positive social context.

These all add up to disrupted academic and social growth.

Interestingly, there may be a physiological perspective to consider when understanding how students may become distracted by certain types of bullying. Researchers hypothesize that the negative effects of inhibiting emotions observed in adults may also be present in children too. For example, when an individual suppresses negative feelings, he or she experiences an increase in cardiovascular and cognitive activity. When children or adolescents strain to control their anger, anxiety, or fear about being victimized by peers, their cognitive systems (e.g., ability to focus, sustain attention, memory, and learning) become taxed and less efficient, resulting in decreased functioning (Conway, 2005; Gross & Levenson, 1997; Richards & Gross, 1999). Adults who experience social conflict at work may be able to empathize with young people in social conflict when the adults recall the amount of mental energy involved with managing their own emotions around negative social experiences and simultaneously being productive at work. In terms of children's and adolescents' school functioning, poor cognitive efficiency can result in disrupted academic and social growth. Again, because of girls' reliance on relationships with others, they are often impacted more negatively than males when they are caught up in relational and social aggression at school (Goldstein & Tisak, 2004).

Unfortunately, the chronic conditions of stress related to relational aggression may have a cumulative negative impact, resulting in poor psychosocial adjustment. Students who are victims of relational aggression may experience a variety of difficulties including the following: (1) internalized suffering associated with anxiety and depression, (2) external behavioral reactions such as agitation, anger, and "acting out," and, in some cases, (3) intrusive memories of negative events that can permeate thoughts and feelings to such an extent as to be labeled posttraumatic stress disorder (Craig, 1998; Crick & Grotpeter, 1996; Crick & Nelson, 2002; La Greca & Harrison, 2005; Rigby & Slee, 1993; Storch & Esposito, 2003). School avoidance may be one by-product of students attempting to cope with intrusive memories or fear of being victimized again by their peers. Given the profound effect of relational and social aggression on intrapersonal development, it is critical for school systems to address instances of this type of bullying so that typical social and academic development can proceed uninterrupted.

PRIMARY PREVENTION PROGRAMS: SUPPORT FOR CHILD DEVELOPMENT

Certainly, the best form of treatment is to prevent problems from ever occurring. Setting up supportive home and school environments that promote healthy emotional, social, and cognitive adjustment is the best way to decrease distress and psychopathology in children and adolescents (Brazelton & Greenspance, 2000). Support programs aimed at increasing a child's communication, assertiveness, anger management, negotiation, and social competence skills are most typical in the preschool years (Brazelton & Greenspance, 2000). As children start to be able to stop themselves (regulate their behavioral responses) at about the age of five, there is less emphasis on emotional and behavioral control skills provided in the classroom. However, it is not until children are about 12 years old that researchers find that emotional (Lane & Schwartz, 1998) and cognitive control (e.g., Piaget, 1932, 1952; Vygotsky, 1962; Woolfolk, 2004), and moral reasoning (e.g., Piaget, 1932, 1952; Kohlberg, 1976; Woolfolk, 2004) are becoming solidified within a child's repertoire of skills. Thus, there can be a lag in developmental support at school, discontinuing support for social skill development far before it would be reasonable to expect these skills to be mastered. In light of No Child Left Behind, it is even more probable that less emphasis is given to programs that are geared toward social and emotional development despite evidence that social and emotional health assists with academic development (Shriver & Weissberg, 2005).

There are few investigations of prevention and intervention programming designed to reduce or eradicate relational and social aggression among students (Crick, 1996). Prevention programming outcomes are notoriously difficult to measure as problems are prevented, and it is not known how many individuals were better off or who avoided a particular behavior due to receiving the support. As such, there is a great deal of backing for prevention programming in theory; however, sometimes it is difficult to fund or enact prevention programming, and very little data has been collected around these outcomes.

Therefore, intervention or acting on a problem that has been identified is much more likely to receive the attention of researchers. Researchers in the Slovak republic sought to decrease aggressive behavior in schools through cognitive support training. They gave 16 10- to 45-minute lessons to individuals (to promote self-acceptance, self-confidence, self-respect, and expression of inner feelings), pairs (to teach cooperation, mutual acceptance, tact, and practice meeting the needs of a partner), and groups (to experience cooperation, helpfulness, sharing, and kindness) of early elementary school children. Sramová (2004) found that intentional support interventions by teachers resulted in a distinct reduction of aggressive behaviors with a significant (p = .001) reduction of indirect or relational aggression. These teachers engaged in discussions with their students about the difference between pro-social behaviors and hostile actions. Teachers gave specific examples of how to be empathic (e.g., perspective taking) and altruistic (e.g., how to be helpful to others). Class discussions were combined with training methods designed to support empathy development and to reinforce appropriate behaviors for both male and female students alike. These findings are consistent with the premise that developmental support or tailored instruction and interactions designed to meet the students at their current skill level and then guide them toward their next level of development, improves children's psychosocial adjustment (Brazelton & Greenspance, 2000; Loudin, Loukas, & Robinson, 2003). For example, a child may understand how she approaches another child who has made her angry; however, if a teacher mentions "being assertive," the student may not understand how these concepts are the same and/or different and may not include that in her behavioral repertoire until she is clear what assertiveness is. Presenting terms at the children's developmental or age-appropriate level means that they are able to understand through words or actions what the concept (assertiveness in this example) looks and sounds like when being practiced and how it is different than other approaches to conflict.

Teachers can directly support discussions about conflict resolution and types of bullying during the course of instruction. For example, teachers can select readings, videos, and class assignments that can facilitate individual reflection and classroom discussions on issues of mutual problem solving and collaboration among students. Books such as *The Recess Queen* by Alexis O'Neill and Laura Huliska-Beith (2002) may be used with young children to promote positive ways of managing bullies. Additionally, it may be feasible for teachers to create assignments that address state-mandated learning and academic standards and address social skills. For example, in young children working on social studies and character development, discussions and role-playing around democracy (everyone has input), voting (making your own choices), and secret ballots (opportunity to speak your own mind with the influence of others) can all be used to model agreement and disagreement about classroom activities. For older students, if an English teacher is covering persuasive writing skills, the teacher could show a clip from the movie *Mean Girls* or another film that features different types of bullying and then ask students to respond in one of two ways. If students want to write from a victim's perspective, teachers can guide the students to write persuasively about the importance of confidence and assertiveness. On the other hand, if students want to write from the perpetrator's perspective, the students could write persuasively about perspective-taking or empathy. In each example, the teacher uses curricula activities to explicitly state expected behaviors at school and uses examples of misbehavior as an opportunity to teach appropriate responses.

> Social Autopsy: Examination of a social error so as to determine the cause in order to prevent it from reoccurring.

SECONDARY INTERVENTION PROGRAMS: SCHOOLWIDE SUPPORT

Secondary-level intervention programs include large scale, school-based, anti-violence curriculums that address social competence through the development of various interpersonal skills. These skills include the development of empathy and perspective-taking, social problem solving, assertiveness, emotional regulation, and anger management. Primary intervention may occur with a particular teacher's class; however, schoolwide programming involves an organized, systemic effort that may include layers of intervention. Those layers may include a clear anti-bullying policy, specific responses from administrators when they receive a bullying referral, schoolwide assemblies, a schoolwide character education program that focuses on specific skills, and peer helpers who educate other students on effective decision making or problem solving related to conflict. Furthermore, schools with a comprehensive anti-bullying program may also require training for faculty and staff to implement a schoolwide curriculum as well as provide opportunities for parents (e.g., speakers at PTO meetings, parenting workshops) to become involved. Although families are the initial training ground for social skills, schools are a second opportunity for teaching or enhancing these skills.

Researchers have identified components of successful school-based programs that increase social competence and decrease the incidence of peer victimization, including the following: (1) early and on-going teaching of social skills throughout the elementary school period—focused on increasing pro-social behaviors—so that all children can master skills appropriate to their developmental level, (2) connecting social-skill instruction and the existing academic curriculum, (3) targeting children who are at high risk for behavioral difficulties before they show distress, (4) actively engaging students so that they develop an attachment to their school, (5) providing small teacher-child ratios, (6) providing regular training to staff, (7) engaging peers and parents, and (8) systematically evaluating the program to determine intervention effectiveness (Leadbeater, Hoglund, & Woods, 2003). Using these benchmarks, researchers have evaluated the effectiveness of secondary interventions.

In 2002, the Second Step Program (middle school/junior high) was evaluated to determine if there was a decrease in aggression and increase in pro-social skills in 714, sixth- through eighth-grade students (51% girls, 49% boys) in five schools in the United States and Canada. The Second Step Program is a classroom-based, social-emotional program designed to prevent aggression by improving upon children's empathy and perspective taking, problem solving, and anger management skills. Children and adolescents are taught to enhance competencies in the areas of emotion regulation, stress management, and problem solving; and many lessons in the curriculum are focused on decreasing or eradicating relational and social aggression. Outcome data showed that when compared to a school without an intervention program, one group of adolescents (second year of junior high) that participated in the Second Step Program showed a decrease in aggression and reported less difficulty using appropriate social skills. Interestingly, these same effects were not observed in sixth-grade students at the same school (Van Schoiack-Edstrom, Frey, & Beland, 2002).

In 2002, eight fifth-grade girls participated in a short-term treatment program designed to reduce relational aggression and victimization called the Friendship Group. The interventions were targeted more to the girls' needs than a general program, but several psychoeducational techniques (e.g., cognitive behavioral strategies, assertiveness training called Brave Talk, social skills, and education focused on victimization) were taught in a group format. Outcome data showed a significant decrease in relational aggression and a significant increase in pro-social and assertive behaviors (O'Donnell, 2002).

In 2003, the Walk away, Ignore, Talk, and Seek help (WITS) program was evaluated to determine if there was a decrease in relational aggression in 432 first-grade students (49% girls, 51% boys) in an urban community in western Canada. The goal of the WITS program is to create classroom, school, and family environments that promote positive behaviors and reduce victimization in children. At the beginning of the school year, all kindergarten to third-grade students are deputized as school police-liaison helpers, and they are charged with the responsibility of helping other children and keeping the school safe. This book-based classroom curriculum is accompanied by a stuffed walrus named Witsup, activity books, bookmarks, pens, pencils, pamphlets for siblings, and recommendations for children's literature that can be used to reinforce WITS's positive messages (Leadbeater et al., 2003). Outcome data showed that when compared to a school without intervention, the WITS program's classrooms showed a decrease in relational victimization from the beginning of first grade until the end of second grade (Leadbeater et al., 2003). Students in these classrooms also showed less behavior problems, fewer emotional problems, and better social competence.

In 2003, kindergarten students participated in a research-informed intervention, which followed the rule, "You can't say; you can't play" to increase pro-social behavior. The program is six to eight weeks and begins with a story about playing with others (e.g., feeling included or left out) and is followed by role-plays and discussions. A classwide positive effect was observed, and socially accepted or popular children began to conclude that playing with a variety of children could be enjoyable (Harrist & Bradley, 2003).

In 2005, a diverse sample (41.2% Latino, 34.3% European American, 19.7% African American, 4.7% other) of 548 third-grade children (49.1% girls, 50.9% boys) participated in the Making Choices: Social Problems Skills for Children program designed to promote social competence and reduce aggression. Interventions focused on improving social information processing (e.g., identifying social beliefs and scripts, weighing social contingencies, recognizing social patterns) and increasing emotion regulation. Outcome data showed that when compared to individuals who did not receive the intervention, participants showed less social and overt aggression and higher social competence and information processing skills than in children in a control group (Fraser et al., 2005).

In 2006, the Social Aggression Prevention Program (SAPP) was evaluated to determine if there was a decrease in social aggression and an increase in positive leadership skills in a sample of fifth-grade girls. Outcome data showed that when compared to a school without intervention, all students participating in the SAPP curriculum demonstrated better social problem-solving skills. For at-risk students who were already showing social problems, teachers reported more pro-social behaviors among SAPP participants (Cappella & Weinstein, 2006).

Finally, Camp Ophelia and Club Ophelia are two programs designed to teach middle school girls how to gain social support and engage in prosocial relationships. This multi-sensory curriculum uses the arts and mentoring to illustrate the ERI model: Educate, Relate, and Integrate. First, girls learn about relational aggression and the negative effects it has upon others. Second, girls relate the concept of relational aggression to incidents in their own lives for the purpose of developing alternative behaviors. Third, the girls integrate the skills learned from the program into their ongoing friendships. In one study, researchers found that 42 adolescent, middle school girls reported positive behavior change after participating in Camp or Club Ophelia, although the changes were not statistically significant (Dellasega & Adamshick, 2005).

There are several other programs that do not yet have data to evaluate their usefulness. However, there are many unique practices that may prove promising. For example, in one program children rotate through hands-on activities in general education subjects (e.g., math, social studies, and science) along with activities in social skills training where students are asked to monitor social cues in their environments to increase social cognitive skills (Bryan & Bryan, 1995; Talbott, 1997). Similarly, *Tootling* was developed to positively alter the classroom environment to focus on pro-social behaviors (Skinner, Cashwell, & Skinner, 2000). In this program peers identify and write down the positive behaviors of one another (e.g., cooperation, helping) and then receive activity-based rewards (e.g., playing an academic game, free reading) for their pro-social behaviors.

These research results are promising as there are a variety of methods that have been shown to be effective in decreasing aggression as well as increasing pro-social behaviors. Because relational aggression is caused by multiple interacting factors, various intervention strategies may prove effective. However, there are two cautions. First, although a "broad-brush approach" has shown to be effective, school personnel still need to be explicit in stating their behavioral expectations for students at their school (Werner & Nixon, 2005). This is especially true for relational aggression where some behaviors do not always violate the school's student code of conduct. For example, student behaviors that provoke a socially hostile environment for others may need to be highlighted as inappropriate in anti-bullying policies.

Caution!

✓ Always explicitly describe the behavior you want.

✓ Always explicitly describe the behavior you do *not* want.

✓ Some students will need tailored interventions (even with good instruction).

Furthermore, secondary interventions may help groups of students on average; however, they are not created to target behaviors of specific students. Students whose maladaptive coping skills are more engrained may not benefit from secondary interventions, and school personnel should not misinterpret these exceptions as rationale not to use secondary programming. Most importantly, individual students who not benefit from secondary interventions may require tailored tertiary interventions.

TERTIARY PREVENTION PROGRAMS: TARGETED INTERVENTIONS FOR STUDENTS

Tertiary intervention is used for specific students who are at risk for engaging in or being victimized from relational or social aggression or are already involved as perpetrators and/or victims. The previous discussion on primary and secondary interventions included the involvement of male and female students, as it may be difficult to separate students based on gender for classroom or schoolwide interventions. For purposes of focusing on the unique needs of girls and female adolescents as outlined in Chapter 1, this section will discuss group counseling and individual counseling for girls. Individualized intervention should be available at the school through the school counselor; however, it will take collaboration with administrators, fellow educators, and parents for these efforts to be effective. For example, administrators who are knowledgeable about the types of support victims and perpetrators need for new skill development are key in making sure that girls who receive disciplinary referrals or those who are seeking support from authority because of their victimization find their way to a counselor. Parents are also an important referral source since the evidence of being involved in relational or social aggression may be reported at home rather than to educators. Unfortunately, when comparing teacher and parent reports of relational aggression, researchers have found that these two groups do not report the same rate or type of relationally aggressive behaviors or overall adjustment difficulties of children (Casas et al., 2006). This is concerning, as quality tertiary intervention will require close collaboration among counselors, teachers, and parents. All three parties can be instrumental in helping bring about change.

Group Intervention

Tertiary intervention may be implemented through individual or group counseling for specific students who need this level of intervention. In Chapter 5, the Goodwill Girls small-group curriculum is presented in detail as an example of a tertiary intervention. Small groups can be an excellent intervention tool as girls are invited to discuss issues of relational and social aggression while also engaging in activities and exercises to help them think more critically about what relational and social aggression is, why it is used, and how individuals (e.g., victims and perpetrators) can cope or learn alternative skills. Because of the pervasiveness of these types of bullying, counselors must remember than many girls have been in both roles at one time. Groups can also be powerful experiences for girls as they are able to relate to one another about similar experiences while also learning strategies for coping with conflict and competition from their peers. With careful guidance from a respected counselor, positive peer pressure can be generated and used to combat practices of relational and social aggression.

Counselors who conduct group counseling as a tertiary intervention should consider initiating a small group intervention when they have identified four or more students who would benefit from a psycho-educational experience targeting relational and social aggression. Group counseling versus seeing each female individually can save time and help to provide a peer circle that will support the new and improved coping skills that come about after participation in the group. When preparing for a group, the counselor must decide on a curriculum that is developmentally appropriate and designed to engage group members with one another. Additionally, the counselor needs to organize the logistics of the group, including number of sessions, the day, and times for each group session, and where the group sessions will be held. If a counselor is unable to use study halls for group sessions, the group sessions should be timed so that students do not miss the same class repeatedly. For example, if a school has a six-period day, the counselor may want to plan the first group session for first period, the second group session for second period, and so on.

> Good Practice: Always require group members to check in with their classroom teachers prior to coming to group. This helps ensure teacher awareness of where the student is and reinforces that students be responsible for any missed class work.

Support from administrators, teachers, and parents is ideal. Therefore, each party needs to be made aware of the purpose of the group as well as all of the logistical information. Asking administrators and teachers for referrals can help identify potential group members as well as helping fellow educational professions feel that they are contributing to the process. If group counseling is not routinely part of a comprehensive school counseling program, consent forms must be sent home to parents to inform them of the group and to solicit their permission for their daughters' involvement. Care should be taken to include information about the student's responsibilities as a group member, and it is good practice for group members also to sign an assent form that outlines expectations of group members. In conclusion, Chapter 5 is devoted to discussing a specific small-group intervention as well as presenting a curriculum that can be followed. Specific facilitation tips are provided for each group session.

> When initiating group counseling as a tertiary intervention, do the following:
>
> ✓ Identify an age appropriate curriculum that is interactive and fun.
>
> ✓ Secure permission and support from the administrator.
>
> ✓ Organize logistical information (number of group sessions, dates, times, location).
>
> ✓ Solicit input from teachers, including student referrals for the group.
>
> ✓ Advertise the group to students (announcements, posters, personal referrals from counselor's office).
>
> ✓ Examine the referrals, including interested students and consider suitability for a particular group.

> ✓ Screen potential group members (have members apply in writing or interview them) and make selections for group membership.
>
> ✓ Secure parent permission from selected participants.
>
> ✓ Secure written commitment and awareness of expectations for the group from all participants.

Individual Intervention

Traditional aspects of individual counseling are applied when considering individualized interventions for girls who are dealing with relational or social aggression. For example, the counselor must first develop rapport with the student. This can be achieved by using active listening, discussing confidentiality, making students aware of the role of the counselor, and using a nondirective approach as the student begins to develop trust and a willingness to be open.

Students who frequently perpetrate relational and socially aggressive acts may immediately become defensive and question the counselor about why she "has to" come to counseling. It is important for the counselor to be honest and maintain a connection with the student. For example, a counselor may respond by saying, "Rita you are right. You do not have to come to counseling. However, I enjoy talking to and getting to know all students at my school. Your teacher is concerned that you are having a lot of arguments with your classmates lately and I am here to help students. So I am interested in understanding how things are for you right now at school and if I can help you."

Victims may be embarrassed by an offer of assistance and may want to simply avoid talking about a topic that brings them much displeasure. If a victim refuses to talk, it is important for the counselor to indicate a desire to help when the victim is ready. For example, "Okay, I can tell you don't want to talk about this, Susan, and I am not going to push you. I just want you to know that you can talk with me if and when you want to. I have met with other students whose friends were giving them a real hard time, and sometimes I have helped. Is it okay if I check in with you in a couple days and see how things are going?"

If a student is coming to a counselor for the first time, it is helpful if the counselor is viewed as a resource in the school that regularly meets with students for a variety of issues. A counselor will gain student trust faster if he or she is a visible, viable professional who is routinely available to students. Furthermore, if the counselor has done classroom guidance lessons or organized schoolwide programming on relational and social aggression, it is more likely that students will seek him or her out for individual counseling sessions associated with these issues.

Various counseling theories may be useful in helping adolescent females examine behaviors associated with being a perpetrator or victim, and two theories will be discussed here. Cognitive behavioral approaches can be used to help a student become aware of the thoughts she is using, examine the impact of these thoughts concerning her feelings and behaviors, and help her make decisions about the types of thoughts she would like to use to feel better. For example, a student being victimized may think, "Everyone hates me," which leads to feelings of sadness and school avoidance. A counselor can help the student recognize this automatic thought, examine whether it is accurate, and reconstruct it to something more accurate such as, "A group of girls in my gym class do not like me and are being mean right now. However, I have friends in my other classes who care about me." Reconstructing the original thought will help the girl to feel less sadness and feel more encouraged about attending school (Ellis, 2001).

For a student who is a perpetrator, she may think, "I heard Traci was talking about me the other day. That is awful, and I am going to get her back!" A counselor can carefully ask what evidence there is to support that another student was talking about her. This may be a risky endeavor as the student may have plenty of evidence. The next line of inquiry from a cognitive behavioral perspective is twofold: Is it more terrible if someone is talking about her, or is she more annoyed by this behavior? If the behavior can be respectfully reframed from "terrible" to "annoying," there will be a decrease in emotional intensity. Counselors using this theoretical approach need to be considerate of the students however irrational their thoughts may seem or be. Additionally, counselors must be patient with the process and consistent in helping students identify their thoughts, as this requires metacognition, a new cognitive skill for many adolescents. However, the promising aspect of this strategy is that students will be able to use these critical thinking skills in all areas of their lives.

Solution-focused theories can also be helpful in working with victims and perpetrators. These approaches are goal oriented, use scaling questions to pinpoint degrees of a phenomenon, and often focus on strengths of the individual, which includes highlighting past attempts at solving problems that were successful (de Shazer, 1985). A counselor using a solution-focused approach will clearly need to understand what a student's goal is and whether or not that goal is within her control. If the victimized student informs the counselor that she wants all of the girls bullying her to be suspended, the counselor will need to ask the student what she, the student, can do to make that happen. Most likely a student will respond that she can't make that happen. If this occurs, the counselor will ask what the student wants that she can achieve through her own power. If the student responds that she wants new friends, a solution-focused approach may involve the counselor asking the student what she has done to make friends in the past or how she has been able to maintain friendships in the past (with exceptions to the current problem). The counselor may also use a scaling question after completing this inquiry. For example, "With 10 being very likely, and one being not likely at all, how likely are you to call your friend Sheila who you have not talked to in a long time?" If the student states that she is at a five on this scale of commitment, the counselor can ask what would need to happen for her to be at a seven. If the student cannot identify any thoughts or feelings that could motivate her more, then the counselor and student can go back to brainstorming other options for making friends or reacquainting with a friend who may lend support. A specific plan should be formulated, and the counselor and student should focus on this plan, complying with it or altering it for effectiveness in subsequent sessions.

For a student who is perpetrating relational and social aggression, a solution-focused approach will work especially well if the student has been reprimanded for problematic behaviors. It is then that a student will want to find ways of dealing with the social dynamics of the school without getting into trouble with school administrators and social milieu. The counselor may help the student focus on strengths (e.g., able to talk to best friend, able to talk openly with mom, able to ignore some things, able to focus on other activities) they have when confronted with stress. After these strengths are uncovered, the counselor can help the student identify specific goals that rely on the strengths. For example, if a student is tempted to spread gossip because she dislikes a particular girl, she can talk to her mom about why she was tempted and why she is having trouble accepting the girl. Obviously, this strategy will be more powerful if the mother is on board with eliminating negative social behaviors. Interventions with parents will be discussed in Chapter 4.

At the present time, there is very limited information about the usefulness of targeted intervention programs, as counselors often do not collect data on individual interventions with students or their parents. Examining the outcomes of tertiary interventions and their theoretical foundations are the next steps in clarifying how a child's specific needs can be addressed most effectively. Specifically, researchers need to determine if targeted interventions alone provide any more impact than broad curricular approaches (secondary intervention). This is important as there is evidence in the literature that demonstrates that relational aggression often decreases among students even when interventions focus on general, pro-social behaviors (Belgrave, Brome & Hampton, 2000). Finally, researchers need to clarify if and when an integrated or layered approach (primary + secondary + tertiary) to intervention is warranted.

CONCLUSION

School personnel have an opportunity to positively influence the lives of children and especially the self-efficacy of young women. Informed school systems addressing the social needs of children increase the student body's ability to focus on academic skills, thus increasing the opportunity for time on task and ultimately real-life successes both socially and academically (Brazelton & Greenspance, 2000). School personnel need to know factual information about all types of bullying, observation and assessment skills, and be aware of the various types of intervention strategies and the type(s) that may best serve their students.

There are many prevention and intervention programs that provide evidence of their usefulness to address the needs of children experiencing relational and social aggression as well as bullying in general. Yet, there are many barriers that impede school systems from implementing such programs. Districts are saturated with academic requirements (e.g., state standards, No Child Left Behind) that tend to override the social needs of students. Greene (2006) argues that only when issues of social justice, human rights, and citizenry secure their place in modern education will stakeholders in schools routinely fund pro-social curriculum for all students. Yet a sense of psychological and physical safety is essential for many students to feel connected to school and fully invested in academic endeavors.

Reflective Questions

✓ Can you identify the school variables that would promote or deter relational or social aggression in the students at your building?

✓ Do administrators and teachers know how to describe relational or social aggression?

✓ Are administrators and teachers aware of the consequences of relational and social aggression?

✓ What is at stake for your students if relational and social aggression is ignored?

✓ What does your administrator need to hear to help her or him support primary, secondary, and tertiary programming to address relational and social aggression?

Strategies for Working With Parents and Teachers

4

Mr. Smith is a school counselor at Westfield Middle School. The principal recently asked Mr. Smith to meet with a seventh-grade student named Toya who in the past two months has been disciplined several times for what the principal referred to as "aggressive incidents." The principal reported that in one incident Toya threatened to "beat up" a student named Larnetta when Larnetta confronted Toya about rumors that Toya wrote on the girls' bathroom wall that Larnetta was a "slut." In another case, Toya refused to allow Danielle to sit at the lunch table with Toya and her friends. Meeting individually with Toya, Mr. Smith explained that if she was interested, he could work with her to help her identify ways she might handle situations differently so that she could avoid getting into trouble with school officials. Toya rather angrily stated that she had no need to talk with him, as there was nothing wrong with her. In an attempt to develop rapport, Mr. Smith asked Toya to share her perspective on what happened in these recent situations. Toya bluntly asserted that the girls should get what was coming to them for messing around in other people's business. When questioned by Mr. Smith, Toya explained that Danielle chose to be thrown out of the group of girls they hung out with when Danielle called Toya's boyfriend. Despite Mr. Smith's efforts to further understand Toya's perspective, followed by him expressing his concern that Toya may continue to get in trouble, Toya refused to talk with him further. Approximately one month later, Toya was again referred to the principal after Danielle alleged to a teacher that Toya and Toya's friends were overheard calling her nasty names in the hallway. Due to the continuance of Toya's social aggression and Toya's lack of interest in individual counseling,

> *Mr. Smith and the principal agreed to involve Toya's parents. At the meeting between the school officials and Mr. and Mrs. Brown, Toya's parents, the couple denied that Toya had made verbal threats or name-called, claiming that they best knew and trusted their daughter. Second, the couple argued that the school's recent focus on decreasing bullying was stupid with Mrs. Brown exclaiming, "Girls will be girls!"*

This chapter focuses on consultation with parents and teachers of students who demonstrate relational or social aggression. Many parents and teachers may have good intentions with their intervention strategies; however, if they do not look at relational and social aggression as a student's demonstration of maladaptive skills that need to be replaced with pro-social skills, some of their efforts may be in vain. Working with parents can present unique challenges for the counselor; however, without this step, girls and female adolescents may not become invested in interventions that promote change, as the dynamics of their families may reinforce relational or social aggression. Sibling relationships are the first opportunity children have to learn and exhibit relationally aggressive approaches to conflict, competition, or expression of anger. Children who do not receive adequate parental support in working through these initial familial conflicts may adopt maladaptive social skills in that context and then transfer those skills to the school environment when they become school age (Crothers et al., 2007).

Obviously, the salience of parent support and guidance does not end when children enter school, and research supports the value of home-school partnerships where parent involvement and bullying are concerned. For example, some forms of parental intervention (e.g., highlighting children's mistakes, commenting on either child's ineffective problem solving, and/or taking on the responsibility of problem solving for their children) may increase relational aggression among siblings. If parents coach their children to manage female sibling conflict (e.g., identify the source of their distress, how to separate their feelings from the words others say, how to pro-socially assert their needs), they may be more likely to deal with conflict assertively and directly. Parents can coach siblings through conflicting social interactions, helping to support independent assertiveness among children who tend to be victims or diminish overpowering another through relational manipulation among children who are relationally aggressive.

WORKING WITH PARENTS OF
RELATIONALLY AGGRESSIVE GIRLS

Working with the parents of relationally aggressive children is critical given that research reveals that there is a significant relationship between parenting and children's use of relational aggression. Research has consistently demonstrated a strong relationship between overt and physical forms of childhood aggression and both highly punitive parenting and negative affect between parent and child (Crick & Dodge, 1994). Some of the parental behaviors that have been associated with higher levels of relational aggression include negative emotion between mother and child (Brown, Arnold, Dobbs, & Doctoroff, 2007; Campbell & Frabutt, 1999), maternal permissiveness (Brown et al., 2007; Sandstrom, 2007), maternal coercion, marital conflict, and lack of parental responsiveness (Hart, Nelson, Robinson, Olsen, & McNeilly-Choque, 1998), highly punitive mothers (Sandstrom, 2007), and low parental monitoring (Penney, 2007). Another parental behavior that has been found to be related to higher levels of relational aggression is what is referred to as psychological control (Casas et al., 2006; Grotpeter, 1998; Penney, 2007), which involves threats of withdrawing love or inducing shame unless a child complies. Parents who are psychologically controlling imply that love and acceptance will not be restored until the child changes his or her behavior (Barber, 1996). Interestingly, this is the same type of behavior that may be exhibited by relationally aggressive girls or young women toward their female friends. Counselors must realize that parents may be used to patterns of relational aggression in the family and may not understand that it can be highly problematic in a school environment.

A realistic, initial goal for counselors working with parents of relationally aggressive girls is to gain at least enough of the parents' support so that they will not undermine teachers or administrators by directly or indirectly implying to their daughter that she does not need to adhere to schools officials' expectations regarding aggression. Parents of relationally aggressive girls may not regard the behavior as a concern because dominance-oriented strategies may be used within their own families. In other words, such behavior may be perceived by parents as normal and effective. Thus, although parents of relationally aggressive girls should be seen as important collaborators with school officials, counselors and teachers may expect such parents to be angry and confused when school officials notify them about their daughter's behavior.

At the initial conference with parents of a relationally aggressive daughter, the school counselor should use a no-nonsense, factual presentation and avoid engaging in questioning, long discussions, or using a tone that invites blame upon the parents. Parents of perpetrators may minimize or deny the incidents. In such situations, it is best that the school counselor or other school officials be prepared to present a narrative description of the incident or incidents and articulate how their daughter's behavior violated the student code of conduct.

Parents of a relationally aggressive girl may be more likely than parents of physically aggressive children to regard their daughter as being a victim rather than an aggressor for several reasons. Relational aggression, in comparison to physical aggression, involves more complex, reciprocal interactions that preclude easy identification of aggressor and victim. In a school context, it is feasible for an adolescent female to be both a perpetrator and victim of relational aggression during a given week. Furthermore, the relationally aggressive girl may have previously complained to her parents about her interpersonal conflicts without including her own aggressive contributions. For example, in cliques of adolescent girls, one or two girls may be temporarily excluded from the group. The daughter may vociferously complain to the parents during the exclusion. However, the group dynamics frequently shift, and the girl who was once excluded may regain closeness within the group without informing her parents. Often this might be achieved by aligning herself with the group in choosing a new girl to exclude without the parents being aware of what their daughter did to regain membership within the group. In cases where the counselor believes that the girl's victimization is partially the result of being involved in the aggression, the counselor might say to the parents, "I imagine that you are probably pretty angry and hurt when you see your daughter in pain like this, and I'm glad that you're sharing you concerns with me. I would like to talk more about how you can help your daughter avoid getting so hurt, and part of helping your daughter may involve helping her to see some of both the good and bad ways that her group of friends handles conflict."

School counselors must gain the trust of the parents of the relationally aggressive student. Such parents may be likely to be aggressive themselves and may look to displace their anger upon school officials. In other words, redirect the focus to another person or topic. The counselor must not take the bait by defensively responding to the misdirected anger but should affirm the parent's anger (e.g., "I can tell that you are frustrated by this situation."). The school counselor should attempt to identify the feelings that lie behind the parent's anger, which may be frustration or confusion, and reflecting such feelings can reduce the parents' emotional intensity and shift the focus to the parents' concern for their daughter. Parents who continue to seem to have little concern about their daughter's relational aggression might be informed in a neutral but concerned tone that such behaviors are often indicative of other psychological and behavioral issues. Relationally aggressive children are at greater future risk for experiencing both internalizing difficulties, including loneliness, depression, anxiety, and somatic complaints and externalizing difficulties, including physical aggression and delinquency (Crick, Ostrov, & Werner, 2006). Furthermore, although relational aggression may actually be associated with popularity at younger ages, the popularity of relationally aggressive children often declines during adolescence (LaFontana & Cillessen, 2002).

Furthermore, school policies against relational and social aggression may also help persuade parents of the situation's importance; however, counselors should not lead with this rationale with angry parents. Once the parents' anger has been reduced, the counselor may shift to more of a problem-solving and developmental perspective in asking the parents what they would like their daughter to learn about relationships and managing conflict. The parents of the relationally aggressive child may struggle in identifying such developmental objectives given that they may not necessarily value egalitarian relationships. For example, a counselor may say to parents, "I hear your concerns that these behaviors may be common for girls, but I think that one of the things that girls at this age are learning about is how to handle conflict where both girls may be angry but can show each other respect in a way that they can work out their differences and still keep their friendships."

The following are goals for the first contact with parents of a girl who is engaging in relational aggression:

✓ Gain at least a modicum of parents' trust.

✓ Avoid implication of blaming parents.

✓ Identify the problematic behavior, identifying which school rules were violated if necessary.

✓ Build consensus regarding what social skill the parents' daughter needs to develop.

School counselors should pursue opportunities to consult with parents of relationally aggressive girls beyond the initial contact given that the research suggests that enduring parent-child relationship patterns may support children's relational aggression. As mentioned earlier, maternal authoritarianism is associated with higher levels of relational of aggression among children (Sandstrom, 2007). Authoritarian parenting is one of the four parenting styles in Baumrind's (1966) well-known framework and is characterized by considerable emphasis on discipline and obedience with little warmth and responsiveness (Baumrind, 1966). In contrast, authoritative parents emphasize rules but are open to reasoning and negotiating with their child and are warm and nurturing. Research consistently reveals that authoritative parenting was associated with the most positive outcomes for children's adjustment, whereas children from authoritarian households are more likely to be anxious and hostile. Children who receive neglectful and indulgent parenting are more likely to lack self-control (Santrock, 2006). In summary, authoritative parents offer both nurturance and discipline whereas authoritarian parents offer discipline but little nurturance. When responding to news that the child is demonstrating inappropriate behaviors at school, an authoritarian parent might respond by using physical punishment or verbal criticism, or such a parent may disregard the issue because he or she does not see aggression as necessarily problematic. In contrast, authoritative parents probably would be more likely to express disappointment with their child regarding the behavior, explain that to their child they expect them to deal with others in a respectful manner, and discuss how the child might avoid relational aggression in similar situations in the future.

In working with authoritarian parents, school counselors should look to both increase the amount of nurturance such parents demonstrate toward their daughters and modify the parents' disciplining style. Such families may rely upon power-oriented strategies in which decisions are based on a fairly rigid hierarchy (e.g., mom makes all the decisions, no questions asked; dad concurs and is mostly disengaged, and the teenage girl must comply without discussion). Parents of relationally aggressive girls may respond to school's concern with one or two ineffective extremes: dismissing the relational aggression as harmless or assuming a harsh punitive stance. Neither approach assists the girl in understanding how to deal more maturely with relationship conflicts. A more authoritarian approach may be developmentally appropriate for families with young children, but in order to facilitate the girl's movement to adolescence and a more egalitarian form of relating, the parents must gradually reduce the power differential in their relationship with their daughter. The parents can be encouraged to share more of their thoughts and feelings regarding their decisions with their daughter and invite their daughter to share her thoughts and feelings concerning family issues. Collaborative decision making between the adolescent and her parents may occur when appropriate. The parents should be encouraged to use active listening skills to understand their daughter's feelings, thoughts, and motivations and should be discouraged from primarily providing advice, dismissing the daughter's thoughts or feelings, or using a shaming or condescending tone.

Such practices help the girl understand the complexity of resolving relational conflict in a collaborative manner and processing the complex feelings and thoughts associated with close relationships. Another way a school counselor can help a parent to lessen a rigid family hierarchy is by encouraging parents to self-disclose to their daughter the parents' own relationship dilemmas from their childhood or adolescence. For example, parents could share with their daughter their specific experiences with managing conflict in their friendship with their best friend, feeling excluded from a group, hearing that rumors were being spread about them, losing a friendship, and so on. Such self-disclosure should emphasize parental disclosure of emotions, as this will both help the girl see her parents as more real people and less of distant, authority figures and help promote the girl's emotional awareness regarding relationship dilemmas. The school counselor might say to the parents, "As your daughter matures, she is learning about having closer friendships and dealing with the complexity of the conflict that goes along with closer relationships. One way that you can be so helpful to her is to help her understand how you thought about and dealt with some of the relationship issues she is dealing with. Can you remember what were some of the similar things you dealt with that your daughter is dealing with now? How did you handle those situations and how did you feel?"

Ways parents exhibiting an authoritarian parenting style may reduce rigid family hierarchy include the following:

✓ Explain reasoning behind parental decisions.
✓ Invite daughter to share her feelings and thoughts about family decisions and relationship conflicts.
✓ Self-disclose how they managed relationship issues during childhood or adolescence.

To increase their child's social problem-solving skills, the parents can be encouraged to invite their child to talk more openly about her peer relationships. This will require more listening on the part of the parents. Parents who have not listened in the past may discover that it may take time for their daughter to learn to trust and realize that they will patiently listen and reserve judgment. First, the parents can help their daughter label her emotions regarding various relationship issues in order to provide their daughter with the language and terms to discuss their concerns with their peers. For example, the parent might say to their daughter, "It sounds to me like you were feeling hurt when you found out that your friend didn't ask you to come over?" or "I wonder if you were feeling annoyed when you thought your friend was making fun of you in front of the others." The parents can also promote their daughter's perspective-taking skills by encouraging her to identify the thoughts, feelings, and wants of her peers. Next, the parents should help their daughter understand what her ideal outcome would be, in other words, what would she like to have happen in the relationship? For example, through such a discussion, the parents might help their daughter realize that she wants to retain a particular friendship, but she also wants to feel comfortable in having other friends without it leading to the respective friend becoming jealous, angry, and hurt. Next, the parents can help their child explore how she might attempt to positively influence the relationship or talk with her friend about these concerns. At this problem-solving juncture, the parents should be encouraged to refrain from pushing their ideas since the goal is to promote the daughter's social decision making. The parents should then help their daughter process the choices and consequences of the various solutions she generated. For example, the parents may help their daughter consider how others may respond to their solutions saying, "We can't exactly predict how people will respond, but what is your best guess as to they will say or do?"

Finally, the parent could even role-play with their daughter her solutions, with the parents playing the children with whom their daughter wishes to communicate. Following the role-play, the parents can encourage their daughter's self-evaluation and also provide their own feedback as well. To encourage their daughter's self-evaluation, the parents can ask, "What do you like that you did during the role play? What might you do a bit differently?" This process assists the child in developing the critical reasoning and communication skills essential for mutually beneficial peer relationships.

The counselor can also encourage the parents to confront their daughter about her acts of bullying while simultaneously communicating some specific messages regarding the nature of bullying. As mentioned earlier, the parents of relationally aggressive girls may present the ends of two extremes by either minimizing the issue or being overly punitive with their daughter. The parents should be encouraged to assume more of a mid-course approach between these extremes and demonstrate disappointment when initially approaching their daughter. The following would be a good example of such a mid-course approach assumed by parents, "I'm disappointed about what the school has told me about your involvement in sending anonymous notes to this girl. I believe that you should know this was hurtful to this girl and not what we expect as parents." Parents should be informed that their daughter is not likely to be open about the issue when initially confronted and that the parents should allow some time before attempting to have an open conversation to better understand their daughter's motivations and perspective. The parents should seek to promote their daughter's awareness of the motivations underlying her relational or social aggression, and such knowledge also helps the parents better understand the area of social development with which their daughter needs assistance. For example, the girl may have resorted to relational aggression as an indirect means to address a conflict with a friend with whom she felt betrayed. This should suggest to the parents that the child is lacking assertive communication skills.

In such a case, the parents may affirm that dealing more openly with conflict is difficult but an essential part of healthy, mature relationships. Most parents will have their own experiences where they feared or avoided interpersonal conflict and should be encouraged to share some with their daughter. Parents may identify for the daughter the incredibly common but ineffective tendency to involve a third person during relational tension to increase their daughter's recognition of such patterns. For example, many people will criticize the person with whom they are angry to relieve their anxiety and develop an ally rather than attempt to manage the conflict more directly with the respective person. This is different from situations in which a person may process the issue with a third party to gain clarity about their thoughts and feelings and solutions for addressing the relationship issue. For girls who frequently refer to other peers' involvement in the respective relational aggression incident, this may indicate that the girl feels unsure about the strength of her peer relationships and feels compelled to conform to peer pressure in order to maintain her social position within the group. In such a situation, parents can help their daughter better understand her definition of friendship and trust to help the girl evaluate which of her friendships are more genuine. Furthermore, such a girl may lack self-esteem, and the parents can remind their daughter of her unique strengths. Other girls may be simply motivated by the excitement and feelings of power that is associated with gossiping and relational manipulation. In such an instance, the parents should affirm that there is something inherently exciting about gossip. However, the parents can help their daughter identify the potential disadvantages of gossip and relational aggression, have her recall how she felt when victimized by others, and how such relational aggression has impacted her peer relationships. For example, the parents might say, "We know that it can be exciting to hear gossip, but we have to remember how we feel when others are gossiping about us, and what such gossip does to our friendships. How has gossip hurt your friendships?"

USING ENACTMENTS WITH PARENTS
OF RELATIONALLY AGGRESSIVE GIRLS

Counselors who have gained trust and rapport with parents of a relationally aggressive child may invite the parents to approach the issue with their daughter in the presence of the counselor during a counseling session. Through the use of what is referred to in structural family counseling as "enactments" (Nichols & Schwartz, 2006), the counselor observes and modifies the parent-child relationship by instructing the parents to engage in specific behaviors while modeling for the parents the tone and type of communication style that is likely to be effective in achieving the directive. For example, the initial instruction for parents who are concerned about their daughter's use of relational aggression could be, "Express directly, right now, to your daughter how concerned you are about what she did to Jennifer." The counselor then observes how the parents approach their daughter, how the daughter responds, and then makes specific suggestions to the parents. For example, the counselor might offer the following supportive but directive enactment, "I hear your anger for what your daughter did, but I'm not sure that your concern is getting through to your daughter. Try right now to get your concern about this situation across to her." Once the parents have more adequately conveyed their concern to the child, subsequent directives might involve directing the parents to find out their daughter's perspectives about the behavior using a softer, more inviting tone. For example, the counselor might say, "I think you have really been able to get your point across to your daughter about why this bothers you, now try to find out how she is feeling about this situation." Enactments can help parents who have an authoritarian style learn to use more open and shared communication with their daughter, which is likely to facilitate their daughter's social problem-solving skills. In summary, parents must learn to use their relationship with their daughter as a vehicle for helping their daughter acquire the various and complex interpersonal skills necessary for more mature relationships, which include managing impulsivity and anxiety, trying to understand the feelings and thoughts of others, evaluating the genuineness of others, and achieving compromise through assertive communication.

WORKING WITH PARENTS
OF RELATIONALLY VICTIMIZED GIRLS

The initial step of working with parents of girls who have been victimized is to join with them by acknowledging the parents' anger, hurt, anxiety, and/or guilt through the use of reflective listening, which also tends to decrease the intensity of the parents' emotion and demonstrate that the school counselor cares and will be active in addressing the problem. The counselor should share with the parents some of the concrete measures the school will use to protect their child in this specific instance of relational aggression, as well as inform the parents of the comprehensive, preventative steps the school is using to promote a respectful environment among students. For example, the counselor might say, "I hear your anger and frustration, and I want you to know we here at the school are also concerned and are working to help your daughter and all students feel safe at school. We want you to know that all of your daughter's teachers are aware of what happened between Jessica and her and that they will be watching the situation closely. Jessica has been disciplined, and her parents were also informed of what happened." The school counselor could also help the parents channel their emotional intensity by becoming involved in the school's efforts to promote a safer climate by joining the Parent-Teacher Association or other school committees that include parents. Such steps are typically effective in diffusing the parents' emotional intensity, gaining their trust, and channeling their energy.

School counselors may want to pursue more long-term involvement with parents who express interest or whose emotional intensity continues to be fairly high. Parents whose child continues to be victimized or socially isolated may also request ongoing assistance. Whereas there is a fair amount of research on the role of parenting in relational aggression, the only study examining parenting behaviors and relational victimization found that parents of victims of relational aggression had higher levels of psychological control (Penney, 2007). Parental psychological control, characterized by threats of withdrawing love and guilt induction (Barber, 1996), has been associated with overprotective parenting, including excessive worrying (Mills, Freeman, Clara, Elgar, Walling, & Mak, 2007). Parental psychological control has also been associated with internalizing problems such as anxiety and depressed moods among both adolescents (Wolfradt, Hempel, & Miles, 2003), and children (Siequeland, Kendall, & Steinberg, 1996).

Parents frequently experience considerable emotional reactivity when first realizing that their daughter is a victim of bullying. Such anxiety often leads parents to seek short-term solutions to eradicate the problem and thus quickly relieve their own anxiety by resolving their daughter's suffering. For example, parents may attempt to "rescue" their daughter by requesting that the school keep their daughter away from the perpetrator(s) by changing shared teachers or classes. The parents may assume considerable responsibility for directly resolving the issue with the offending child, which may include aggressively confronting the perpetrator or their parents. This is called "overfunctioning."

Overfunctioning: "Doing things for others that they could do for themselves, which includes advice giving, knowing what is best for others, talking more than listening" (Gilbert, 1992, p. 67)

It is easy to understand why a parent would respond in this manner; however, parents who repeatedly overfunction do not permit their daughter to develop her own coping skills. Another way that parents may attempt to remove the child from painful social situations is by considerably increasing the amount of the time they spend with their daughter, thus removing their daughter's need to find emotional closeness with peers. Such efforts remove what the parents may see as the cause of their child's distress but limit the child's social development with peers. An extreme example of this may be changing their daughter's school.

Ways parents may overfunction for a daughter who is a victim of relational aggression include the following:

✓ Insist that school change their daughter's or the perpetrator's classes/teachers.

✓ Aggressively confront the perpetrator or the parents of the perpetrator.

✓ Considerably increase the time they spend with their daughter, not leaving room for daughter to develop relationships with peers.

What Happens When Social and Relational Aggression Is Not Addressed?

There are a variety of approaches that school counselors can use to help parents of victimized girls. One of the first steps is to help parents recognize how they have been impacted by their daughter's victimization. Such parents often do not realize that they are experiencing considerable emotional intensity or extreme feelings, which are impacting how they are viewing their daughter and her needs. For example, as mentioned earlier, the parent who insists that the school remove their daughter from a class to separate her from the perpetrator or perpetrators may not realize that this may produce some unfavorable consequences. The counselor can help parents own their emotional reactions by first normalizing their reactions, sharing that many parents find it painful to know that their child is being harmed and asking the parents, "Knowing your child has been hurt is hard, and I wonder how you are feeling and thinking?" This will encourage parents to talk or process the situation rather than exhibit a knee-jerk reaction. Next, the counselor will help the parents step outside their relationship with their daughter to examine how their reactivity may be impacting the way they are relating to their daughter. The school counselor can use "process-oriented questions" (Bowen, 1978) by having the parents think about their cognitive, emotional, and behavioral responses while interacting with their daughter and her subsequent reactions. Examples of process-oriented questions include the following: "What do you notice about your thoughts and feelings when you think about what your daughter is dealing with at school?" and "When your anxiety increases, how does it impact the way you talk with your daughter?" The emotional process can also be demonstrated through a graphic display. The school counselor may draw two overlapping circles, shading the part that overlaps, explaining how it represents the emotional fusion that often occurs in families, such as when a child is experiencing difficulties. This fusion occurs when the parent is unable to have feelings that are independent of the child's and vice versa. The visual contrast would be two adjacent circles symbolizing the process of raising a daughter who can independently manage her emotions and identify her own goals and solutions while also being close to her parents.

The counselor should inform parents that although such emotional reactivity is common, it interferes with the ability of the parents to think more objectively about their daughter's developmental needs, and contributes to family tension that the child absorbs, thus impacting the daughter's ability to think clearly about her problems and issues. For example, the parent who is frustrated about learning that her daughter is being victimized at school, may carry this intensity home and unconsciously allow it to impact the way she talks with her husband (e.g., tense and distracted), which increases frustration between the parents, thus contributing to an anxious environment at home that further impacts the daughter. The school counselor can help the parent explore coping mechanisms to reduce emotional intensity or manage emotional intensity. Or the counselor can even directly suggest common stress management techniques, such as exercise, positive or realistic self-talk, having good friends to talk to, and so on.

Reducing the parents' anxiety increases their capacity to objectively understand the developmental needs of their daughter. Research suggests that victims of relational aggression report higher levels of loneliness, depression, and lower global self-worth (Prinstein et al., 2001). Children who are persistently socially isolated may be attractive targets, as perpetrators recognize that these children are not likely to receive assistance from peers. Acquiring friends may reduce such children's vulnerability and help children manage the pain of victimization. Prinstein et al. (2001) found that children who were victims of relational aggression but reported higher levels of close friendship had fewer symptoms of depression and delinquency than victimized children who lacked such social support.

Through consultation, speaking at PTA meetings, and conducting parent workshops, counselors can help parents understand the crucial role they play in promoting their son or daughter's social development and self-confidence. Counselors can explain to parents that given their privileged position as parents, they have considerable insight into their child's weaknesses and potential strengths in connecting to peers. To encourage the parents to adopt more of a developmental perspective in viewing their child, the school counselor may ask the parents, "What might be those social or relationship skills that you think your daughter needs to acquire at this point in her development?" Such a question can shift the parents' exclusive focus upon the pain stemming from the victimization and punishing the accused to more of a solution-oriented perspective, hopefully leading the parents to identify their daughter's developmental needs, whether they be enhanced perspective taking, assertiveness, taking risks to connect with others, understanding her characteristics that make her potentially attractive to peers, and so on.

Parents typically have significant insights regarding their daughter's social difficulties, and counselors can consult with the parents in developing approaches that are specific to the daughter. Or if parents appear to be lacking insight regarding their daughter's social difficulties, counselors can share what they believe is likely to be helpful for the daughter. For example, parents might see their daughter as lacking the self-confidence to approach peers, and research suggests that most socially isolated children who have a fairly long history with social rejection (Boulton & Underwood, 1992) often feel hopeless and are no longer attempting to connect to others. Parents can encourage their daughter's risk taking in social situations. Parents might help their daughter replace negative self-statements, often called self-talk, with more positive self-statements, reminding the daughter of her strengths and what she has to offer as a friend, whether it is humor, intelligence, compassion, or kindness. A book that parents may find helpful in teaching their child to think differently is Bloch and Merritt's (1993) *Positive Self-Talk for Children.* Parents may remind their daughter of previous situations or tasks about which their daughter was initially reluctant (e.g., approaching a new child) but eventually were successful (e.g., making a new friend). Furthermore, parents can model social risk taking by sharing how they managed their own social anxiety during childhood and adolescence. Unfortunately, the initial attempts of socially isolated children may not yield immediate results in terms of acquiring friends as research suggests it takes quite some time for unpopular children to change their level of social desirability (Boulton & Underwood, 1992). In such cases, parents should encourage their daughter to reward herself for such positive risk taking as opposed to overly focusing on the results of their efforts. For example, the parent could say, "I am proud of you for trying a new way to connect with others, and I think you should feel proud of yourself too."

Goals in consulting with parents of daughter who is a victim of relational aggression include the following:

✓ Join with parents by acknowledging their concerns and emotions.

✓ Help parents identify how they can manage their emotional intensity.

✓ Help parents identify specific relationship skills that would promote daughter's social development and how they can promote the acquisition of those relationship skills.

USING ENACTMENTS WITH PARENTS OF RELATIONALLY VICTIMIZED GIRLS

Enactments enable a counselor to observe how the parents both assist the girl's problem solving and support the girl with the pain of victimization. The counselor could initiate the enactment by asking the parents to talk with their daughter about her victimization. Overprotective parents might start by trying to problem solve for their daughter telling her how she could protect herself, get "over it," or make new friends. Or the parents might attempt to nurture their daughter by relying exclusively on physical affection, which is developmentally appropriate for very young children but less so with older children. The counselor looks to modify the structure of the parent-child interactions by reinforcing developmentally appropriate parenting behaviors and blocking less developmentally appropriate parenting behaviors. For example, if the parents start by immediately problem solving or simply expressing concern through physical affection, the school counselor can say, "Mrs. Johnson, I'm so glad that you want to help your daughter with this issue; please try find out what your daughter is thinking or feeling about this issue." Or the counselor could instruct the parents to find out from their daughter what type of help she would like from her parents, such as, "Ask your child what she needs from you at this time." To help promote their daughter's social development, parents can be directed by the counselor to ask their daughter about her ideas concerning how to develop friends. The counselor would block the parents' attempts to solve the problem for their daughter through anxious advice giving. In essence, the counselor is teaching the parents to use active listening skills in relating to their daughter, which can improve the parent-child relationship and provide the parents with the essential skills for promoting their daughter's critical reasoning.

CONSULTING WITH TEACHERS

When intervening with girls experiencing relational and social aggression, teachers need to be aware of whether their approaches in and out of the classroom reinforce the roles of victim and perpetrator. Do educators solve problems for children, thus trumping new skill development, or do they pose questions that help students think about what they are doing, help them analyze the situation, and then determine if their expectations are reasonable? For example, rather than immediately disciplining a student or students, teachers may instead engage the children in dialog through questions such as, "How can you be a friend to others?" "How can you talk to someone about your feelings of being left out?" "Who is in control of your emotions?" and "Is it reasonable to believe that you and your friends will never argue?" It may be difficult to pose these questions when students are distressed or demonstrating strong emotions; however, engaging in dialog versus solving the problem for them is the best way to create or enhance new conflict resolution skills (Updegraff, Thayer, Whiteman, Denning, & McHale, 2005).

CONSULTING WITH TEACHERS IN WORKING WITH GIRLS WHO USE RELATIONAL AGGRESSION

Teachers may have difficulty identifying relational and social aggression, particularly in comparison to more overt forms of aggression, given its more subtle nature. Counselors can conduct workshops for teachers in which they define the nature and various forms of bullying, symptoms of victimization, and identify intervention strategies for teachers. If school counselors cannot justify doing inservice workshops on relational and social aggression only, they may include this information under a broader workshop on the various types of bullying. Research suggests that the frequency of physical aggression and relational aggression are similar among children and adolescents (e.g., Coyne et al., 2006), and it is not feasible for teachers to address each specific instance. Rather, counselors might encourage teachers to intervene with children who demonstrate a consistent pattern of relational or social aggression.

Counselors can train teachers to have one-on-one conversations with perpetrators by demonstrating such interactions through role-playing with teachers. In first approaching a perpetrator, the teacher should be encouraged to be firm, immediately explaining to the girl that the teacher is talking with her due to her inappropriate behavior. The teacher should subsequently identify which classroom or school rule (hopefully relational and social aggression is mentioned in the school rules) has been violated as well as discuss the corresponding consequence. Teachers are more likely to gain the trust of the perpetrator by immediately identifying the relational aggression and the consequence since a straightforward delivery assures the girl that she will not be trapped into a falsehood by asking the perpetrator for her version of events. Thus, teachers should collect evidence from other student witnesses or participants prior to meeting with the perpetrator. For example, a teacher could state to a perpetrator, "Barbara, I am talking with you right now because I'm upset about how you acted toward Juanita. I have talked with several students who told me that you and your friends agreed to no longer be friends with Juanita." Teachers may want to have a mechanism for ongoing discussion about relational or social aggression or other types of bullying with their students by have a problem drop box where students describe the problem for the teacher on paper if the student is unsure about directly approaching the teacher. This will assist the teacher in gathering information and knowing which students are engaging in relational and social aggression according to their peers. Finally, the teacher should also inform the perpetrator that other teachers and school staff will be notified of the incident to prevent such behaviors from continuing.

When working with the perpetrator, it is important for the teacher to subsequently transition to using a more caring and concerned tone, as the objective is to assist the perpetrator to nondefensively evaluate whether her behavior is meeting her goals. Some perpetrators will genuinely appear to suddenly realize the inappropriateness of their behavior and express both remorse and apparent confusion as to what motivated them to engage in such behaviors, which might be seen as a testament to the unconscious or instinctual tendency of this type of bullying. Again, research suggests that relational aggression is actually positively associated with popularity during the elementary years, which may explain how use of these behaviors is socially reinforced (LaFontana & Cillessen, 2002). Teachers might affirm the perpetrator's strengths and popularity to help her realize that relational and social aggression may be unnecessary to achieve her desire for friends or social status and also explain that relational aggression can be risky as peers may be less tolerant of such behavior when they move on to high school. For example, the counselor could encourage teachers to state something similar to the following: "Jennifer, I think you know that a lot of the other students look up to you and admire your intelligence and outgoingness. It seems to me that you are worried about having or losing friends, and I do not think that really is something you need to worry about, as you seem to have a lot of friends. I'm concerned that as you get older, other students will be more likely to get angry if you tell them not to be friends with someone else just because you are mad at that person." As the teacher gains the trust of the perpetrator, the teacher can raise the issue of concern for others or perspective taking, encouraging the child to consider what the victim was feeling and what restitution may be owed. The counselor may encourage teachers to ask perpetrators questions such as, "What do you think Latisha was feeling when she heard you whispering with the girls about her?" and "What do you think was going through her mind?"

Steps for teacher when confronting a girl who is using relational aggression include the following:

✓ Share evidence that indicates that school/classroom rules have been violated.

✓ Explain that the girl's parents and other staff will be notified.

✓ Help the girl examine if relational aggression is effective in achieving her wants.

✓ Encourage the girl to identify with the victim's feelings and thoughts.

Counselors can also help teachers establish a classroom environment that discourages relational aggression. Studies have found that lower levels of aggression are associated with students who have a sense of belonging or a connection to their peers and the class (Grossman, 2000; Shechtman, 2002). Teachers should possess the characteristics associated with what research suggests is the most effective form or parenting, an authoritative style, in which there are clear and high expectations, as well as caring and interest for the child (Santrock, 2006). At the beginning of the school year, the teacher should establish the classroom rules collaboratively with students, which should include the expectation that students are to treat each other respectfully, communicate honestly, and resolve conflicts in a healthy manner. Counselors may introduce teachers to Glasser's (1969) concept of open classroom meetings that involve regularly scheduled sessions when all of the students and the teacher meet to discuss, in a nonjudgmental fashion, important issues in the class, particularly relationships among students. The meetings provide students with an opportunity to learn the essential skills of communication, including sharing their own thoughts and feelings, understanding the thoughts and feelings of others, and practicing thinking and brainstorming in a group. The teacher emphasizes effective communication by modeling and reinforcing assertive communication and blocking put-downs, blaming, speaking over each other, or sharing that is not relevant to the issue. The class should be arranged in a circle to enable students to see each other, and the teacher is part of the circle. The teacher should set a designated time period to ensure that students do not seek to extend the meetings to avoid other academic tasks. A recommended time period for younger students is ten to twenty minutes and thirty minutes for older students. Adolescents can also benefit from talking about classroom or peer dynamics openly, particularly if those dynamics are interfering with the delivery of class content or focus of the students. Emmett and Monsour (1996) found that students who participated in open classroom meetings reported improvements in relating to others, listening, communicating feelings, and solving problems. Despite the mandate for modern teachers to emphasize content and standardized test scores, it is easy to recognize how the creation and maintenance of a safe, positive classroom climate ensures that students are free to use their cognitive resources for learning.

CONSULTING WITH TEACHERS IN HELPING RELATIONALLY VICTIMIZED GIRLS

Counselors should help teachers understand that helping relationally victimized girls may involve both short-term and long-term interventions. Short-term interventions refer to dealing with specific instances of relational and social aggression. Long-term interventions involve promoting the social development of victims both to decrease their attractiveness to perpetrators and to provide a source of social support (e.g., circle of friends) to manage the pain associated with victimization. Since students may be unlikely to report their victimization because they fear exacerbation of the problem or retribution, it is important for teachers to attempt to relieve the anxiety of victims. Teachers should inform the victim that whatever she decides to reveal will be held in confidence, explaining to the girl, "I understand that you might be worried that person who hurt you may find out that you talked me, and I want you know that I will not tell that person that you spoke with me." Helping the victim to identify and affirming her feelings about the victimization helps to develop a girl's trust. The teacher can instill hope for a child whose victimization may be ongoing for a considerable length of time by sharing that he or she has had success in dealing with past student incidents that involved bullying. Victims often internalize the aggression, believing that they are somehow responsible or deserving of the disrespect. Therefore, the teacher should help the girl realize that she is not responsible for the victimization and that the teacher will do everything in his or her power to promote a safe classroom environment. For example, the teacher could say, "Latisha, I know you told me that you are wondering what you have done to get picked on so much, but I want you know that I think it is important to remind yourself that you haven't done anything wrong and that it is these girls who are being inappropriate by being mean to you."

After collecting evidence, the teacher should explain in detail to the victim how the teacher will use the information and if possible, secure the victim's permission to break a confidence if necessary. Teachers should take every precaution so that this process does not "re-victimize" the victim again. Proceeding may include meeting with witnesses and the alleged perpetrator(s), punishing the perpetrator(s), and notifying other teachers so that they more closely observe the involved students. The teacher may have the victim identify other students who are not friends of the victim or the perpetrator who may have observed the events in question, explaining to the victim that these witnesses will not be informed that they were named by the victim as a possible observer. Often the victimization has been occurring for several months, and thus the victim can readily name other students who have observed the events in question. Finally, the victim should be encouraged to notify the teacher if the relational aggression continues.

Counselors can help teachers promote the social development of victims. Teachers often are the adult who most frequently observes a girl's interactions with peers, and thus have considerable insight regarding the girl's specific response patterns in social situations, which can be invaluable to the parents and counselors when conducting individual counseling with victims. Although victims of relational aggression are not responsible for their victimization, often, they may unwittingly contribute to their social isolation. Girls who have not been successful socially often adopt defense mechanisms to manage their sadness and frustration. Some girls may use sarcasm when interacting with peers, which peers may perceive as rudeness. Other girls may be withdrawn or unresponsive during peer interactions, as their hopelessness and/or cautiousness prevents them from accurately perceiving the intentions of other children. Sometimes girls might communicate to peers that they are too eager for friendship in that they are willing to assume a submissive position for the sake of friendship. But this can lead peers to distance themselves as they sense the victim's desperation. Teachers can help the girl identify her defenses by processing social interactions with the victim, asking her to evaluate which of her peers' behaviors does she think helped them to connect with others and which may be have been less effective. For example, counselors can train teachers to ask such questions as, "What do you do that you think helps you feel more connected with others?" and "What do you think you do that might get in the way of being connected with others?"

Teachers also often have considerable insight concerning the varying levels of social status and cliques among the students and thus may be more able to identify children who are more likely to respond the friendship overtures of the socially isolated girl. Socially isolated girls, partially as a consequence of their ostracism, may have difficulty identifying the status hierarchy of a peer group and thus may seek out highly popular peers who are less likely to respond to the socially isolated girl's initiation of friendship. The counselor can encourage the teacher to explore with the socially isolated girl, who they believe is likely to be looking for a friend, has lots of friends, and may not have "room for more friends." Teachers may ask such socially isolated girls, "Who are some girls whom you might like to be friends with whom you think might also want to be friends with you? What tells you that they might be interested in being friends?" Furthermore, teachers can also be encouraged to use this knowledge of social hierarchy by assigning the social isolated girl to work in groups of students who have similar levels of popularity and interests.

Long-term strategies counselors can encourage teachers to use to promote the social development of girls who are frequent victims of relational aggression include the following:

✓ Help the girl become more aware of her strengths and friendship qualities.

✓ Help the girl identify others who would likely respond to friendship overtures.

✓ Encourage the girl to use risk taking in identifying and trying out skills for making friends.

✓ Assign the girl to academic task groups that include other girls who have similar interests and levels of popularity.

CONCLUSION

Working with parents and teachers is an invaluable step in intervening in relational and social aggression. Counselors should seek out opportunities to support parents and teachers one-on-one (e.g., individual meetings) as well as on a systemic level (e.g., parent workshops and teacher trainings). Specific strategies for addressing perpetrators and victims are mentioned in hopes of providing counselors with practical strategies for consulting with parents and teachers.

Goodwill Girls   5

A Small-Group Curriculum

"I used to be aggressive—but now I am really assertive . . . I just tell people what I think."

—C., 14 years old

"And like sometimes if you think of something right then, you need to like step back and just think about how you are going to say it 'cause you could put it a different way and make it seem nicer or not as rude. You just have that anger right then, and you want to just burst out and say it—but then you need to step back and rethink it."

—A., 14 years old

"Like last week my friend said something about what I was wearing . . . they were making fun of me and stuff, and I was using passive aggressive, and I went to my other friend, and I was like telling her how I was like mad and stuff about what she said. I don't want to like . . . I still like her, and I didn't want to say anything mean—but I was just mad over it."

—R., 14 years old

"I just plain out tell them what I think. Most girls in our school are passive aggressive because they cannot deal with the fact that . . . like . . . what the people would think because they have said what is on their mind. And that really bugs me a lot because people need to say what's on their mind., There would be less fighting and less confusion in this school and less people going to the school counselor if they just all spoke their mind and said how it is! Or if someone tells you a secret—just keep your mouth shut!"

—J., 14 years old (Quotes taken from the next to last session in a Goodwill Girls group)

USING GROUP COUNSELING
WITH VICTIMS AND PERPETRATORS

The previous two chapters outline interventions for schools and specifically how to work with parents and teachers. This chapter will focus specifically on how counselors can intercede with pubescent or adolescent females who are engaging in and/or are victims of relational and social aggression through the use of group counseling. The Goodwill Girls small-group curriculum is one example of a psychoeducational group that may be helpful to girls at risk for relational and social aggression. It is important for counselors to remember that many girls may have experienced both the perpetrator and victim role at some point. This group curriculum was developed to provide a structured framework to assist adolescent females in developing healthy skills for relating to one another and resolving conflict in a constructive manner. Remillard and Lamb (2005) found that a common coping strategy for victims of relational and social aggression is to seek social support from others. Additionally, they found that 40% of their research participants who were victims of this manner of bullying maintained their friendships with their aggressors and reported being "close" to those persons.

A group experience may be more powerful than an individual intervention or one-on-one counseling as adolescent females are given an opportunity to listen and learn from one another in a safe, supportive, structured environment. Furthermore, because of the psychoeducational nature of the group, victims and perpetrators will be able to think about what constitutes a healthy friendship and healthy approaches to conflict resolution. Some friendships have enough qualities that they are easily maintained after a conflict occurs. Girls must also learn to recognize when it is unhelpful to maintain relationships with individuals if it involves an ongoing emotional expense to themselves and their emotional well-being.

Within a small group atmosphere, Yalom and Leszcz's (2005) therapeutic factors may emerge, including altruism (an opportunity to help others through one's own contributions), universality (being reassured that a girl is not the only person experiencing problems with friends and the thoughts and feelings that accompany such experiences), installation of hope (hearing about how others have successfully worked through conflict with friends), and social learning (hearing about how others have handled conflict and adopting those practices for one's own, as well as receiving immediate feedback from peers in the group). These by-products of the group experience are particularly powerful among teens as their peers possess much power in shaping or reshaping their thoughts and behaviors. Prinstein et al. (2001) found that friendships serve as a protective factor for individuals being victimized. Therefore, participating in a structured, supportive group where relating to others effectively is the goal, may also help to interrupt a downward emotional spiral toward longer term psychosocial maladjustment.

The Goodwill Girls Curriculum consists of ten sessions appropriate for pubescent or adolescent females ages 10 to 16; however, the curriculum can certainly be shortened or lengthened to accommodate a school schedule. In addition, the group facilitator needs to be flexible enough to honor the pace at which the group is moving, being careful to not move on to different topics or activities unless the group is ready. The curriculum follows the elements of group development, honoring the introductory, transition, working, and termination stages. Therefore, the sessions are presented in a sequential order that will allow the group to move through each of these stages. Ideally, there should be no more than twelve group members to help ensure that each member has an opportunity to participate in group sessions on a regular basis. Additionally, this group should be a "closed" group, meaning group membership does not change, and new members are not added. Accumulating new members can interfere with the group's ability to develop trust and cohesion, two characteristics that are certainly needed when tackling topics such as relational and social aggression. A closed group allows the members to develop a sense of safety, security, and predictability that ultimately aids in the group experience. Group sessions, as listed, take approximately 40 minutes each.

Counselors facilitating the group should screen group participants. For example, two girls who have powerful personalities and a particularly contentious relationship with one another should not be placed in the same group as this will impact the perceived safety of the group for both females and ultimately the other group members. Additionally, group facilitators will also want to be sure to include at least one to two group members who have strong interpersonal skills, possessing the ability to be assertive and give honest feedback to others. These members can model appropriate behaviors and assist with suggesting ways to manage relational and social aggression. Girls should not be forced to participate in a group intervention; however, the group facilitators, while screening or attempting to solicit group members, should clearly articulate the potential benefits of the group experience. Often times, reluctant members grow more committed after participating in one to two sessions.

Consider this: Most of the group activities may be altered and used as classroom guidance lessons with male and female students. Attempt to incorporate visual, auditory, and kinesthetic components to keep the class engaged and on task. Open discussion may be used with the entire class, or the class can be broken up into small groups to complete these tasks.

The following is an outline of the ten group sessions. This group curriculum was piloted in the fall of 2007 with twelve eighth- and ninth-grade girls in a rural junior/senior high school (7th–12th grades) in the northeastern United States. The group was cofacilitated by the school counselor and one of the researchers (employed as a faculty member at a local university). Eleven of the group members were white, and one group member was African American. Following each session outline, there are specific notes for facilitators to consider when conducting this particular group session. The notes are based on the facilitators' reflections on the group sessions.

THE GOODWILL GIRLS SMALL-GROUP CURRICULUM

Session 1: Introduction

1. During the first session, the group facilitator should introduce herself and welcome the girls to the group. Group members should be wearing name tags to help everyone learn names quickly.

2. Introductions: The group members will introduce themselves to the group using a name game. Each group member will select a word that describes her and starts with the first letter of her first name (e.g., "mellow Mary"). Each group member will repeat the names and words used by previous group members.

3. After the introductions, the group facilitator will discuss what a group is and how it is different than a class or being in a classroom. This is especially important for girls who have never been group members before.

4. In an attempt to get the group members used to the idea of talking, the group facilitator will do a "go around." The facilitator will select a group member to begin and the direction in which the group will go in responding to the prompt "Tell the group one thing about yourself." Each group member will participate including the group facilitator when it is her turn.

5. The facilitator will ask the girls to think about how they would like the group members to work together during the group sessions. The facilitator may do this by asking the girls what would need to happen in the group for group members to feel as if they could trust one another. The facilitator will then ask the group members what rules they would like to have for their group. After hearing various responses while brainstorming the group rules (use silence to keep them talking and sharing), the group counselor will record the group rules on a sheet of newsprint and suggest

any additional rules that may be useful for group process. If confidentiality is not addressed by the group members, the group facilitator will discuss this rule specifically. The facilitator will ask a group member to read through the list of group rules.

6. The group facilitator will then introduce the "I Treasure" icebreaker activity (see Appendix). Each girl will complete the worksheet and share her top five with the group. To initiate group processing or discussion, the group counselor will point out similarities between the group members and ask group members what they think of the observations. If "friends" is mentioned as a treasured item (which is typically the case with this age-group), the counselor will ask the group members to discuss why this is a value for many group members.

7. In conclusion, the group facilitator will use another go around and ask the group members to name one thing that they liked about the first group session.

Facilitator Notes: It may be tempting to rush through Session 1 or to start the group with the psychoeducational activity in Session 2; however, each aspect of the first group session as outlined serves a purpose in developing healthy group norms such as each group member contributing, allowing group members to develop and take ownership of group rules, and engaging in a structured activity that is then discussed openly with the group members. These procedures help set the stage for future group sessions where group members are expected to discuss their thoughts and feelings about the topics. Finally, group members may lack confidence in this particular group session and may respond with "I don't know." It is important for group facilitators to balance encouragement (e.g., "Would you like a minute to think? Are you sure you do not have a response?") with allowing group members to contribute without being forced or only when they are ready (e.g., "Okay, let's move to the next person"). It may take time for the group members to trust the group and begin sharing their ideas. If several group members remark that they "do not know," it is important to ask the group, "What do you think will happen if many of the group members do not contribute to this discussion?" Using strategic silence will sometimes help group members understand that the group facilitator will not accept total responsibility for keeping the group moving or engaged.

Session 2: Keeping and Losing Friends

1. The group facilitator will begin the group by welcoming group members back and asking the girls to do a go around by repeating their names for the group and name one thing they remember from the previous session.

2. The group rules should be on display, and the group facilitator will ask one girl to read the group rules.

3. The group facilitator will then announce that the topic for the group is conflict with friends or acquaintances. If several of the girls named "friends" in the "I Treasure" activity, the group facilitator can remind the girls that they named friends as an important concept they value. The facilitator will then ask the group to engage in a brainstorming activity to think about what they do to make and keep friends, and what they do to lose friends. The group should brainstorm what they do to make or keep friends first (two columns on a newsprint page or white board).

4. Discussion: The group facilitator will then ask questions to facilitate discussion. Processing questions may include the following:

- Why do you think girls are willing to make friends or do things to keep friends?
- Are these behaviors difficult to do? If so, why?
- Why do you think girls engage in the "losing friends" behaviors?
- Are these behaviors difficult to do? If so, why?
- How do girls learn to make or keep friends?
- How do girls learn to do things that cause them to lose friends?
- What are the consequences of losing friends?

5. Group members will then look at the "Unhealthy Friends" handout and put a star in each box that reflects a behavior that a friend has done to them. Group members will then be asked to put a check mark beside each behavior that they have demonstrated with a friend. The group will discuss these behaviors and why they are *unhealthy* examples of what friends may do to one another.

6. For homework, the group facilitator will ask the girls to "catch" themselves engaging in behaviors that help them keep or lose friendships between this group session and the next. They will be asked to report these behaviors at the beginning of the next group session.

7. The closing go around will include the girls responding to the prompt "One thing I learned in group today is . . . ."

Facilitator Notes: It is important to link group sessions together; therefore, that is why it is suggested that group facilitators help group members warm up by reflecting on what occurred in the previous session and how to prepare themselves for the next session. The facilitator may want to define brainstorming *if the girls seem unsure about how to proceed in the session. The facilitator should emphasize that group members should feel free to think of ideas, as brainstorming does not include an assessment of whether the idea is "good" or "bad." If the group facilitator discovers that the girls are having difficulty with one person talking at a time, the facilitator may want to introduce a talking stick or tangible item that the girls can hold when each person takes a turn. During the discussion portion, the group facilitator may need to remind group members that only the person holding the item should talk. Stuffed animals work well. After introducing the talking-stick method, it should be used in each subsequent session when the group is discussing or processing group content. Finally, allow enough time for the closing go around as group members need a chance to think about and name what they are learning in the group experience. This activity also helps reinforce that the point of group is to learn.*

Session 3: Naming

1. The group facilitator will begin the group by welcoming members back and asking the girls to discuss their homework.

2. The group rules should be on display, and the group facilitator will ask one girl to read the group rules.

3. The group facilitator will inform the girls that they will learn about relational aggression today as well as different approaches to conflict.

4. The group facilitator will distribute the "Relational Aggression Organizational Map" (see Appendix) and have one group member read through the examples of how a person can display relational aggression through behavior.

5. The group facilitator will then ask the group to discuss how relational aggression fits in with keeping or losing friendships (the brainstorming activity from the previous session).

6. The group facilitator will briefly explain how relational aggression is a way that girls try to address problems or conflicts that they are having with each other.

7. The facilitator will distribute the "Maria and Tara" worksheet (see Appendix) and ask group members to read the scenario silently as one group member is asked to read it aloud.

8. The facilitator will then ask the group members to respond to questions one, two, and three.

9. The facilitator will then ask the group members to discuss what they think Tara should do. (Use the talking stick if necessary).

10. The facilitator will then ask four different group members to read the definitions for *aggressive, passive, passive-aggressive,* and *assertive.*

11. The group will close by the facilitator doing a go around and asking group members to state what they would do if they were Tara in the scenario. The facilitator will collect the Maria and Tara worksheets.

Facilitator Notes: If the group members do not do their homework, ask the group members to think about scenarios with their friends that have occurred between sessions and how the group members responded to the scenarios. Questions can be posed about the effectiveness of group member behavior in the scenarios (e.g., You told me that you and your friend were in an argument this week. I am wondering if what you did during the fight caused you to keep or lose this friend). This session is more structured than the previous sessions as it follows two specific worksheets. If group members appear to be disengaged during some of the content, it is appropriate to ask specific group members to state what they think about the information. Calling on group members should be done to invite members to stay active, not to "punish" group members who appear bored. The facilitator does not want to develop a group norm in which group members who are in trouble are the ones that participate.

Session 4: Pros and Cons

1. The group facilitator will begin the group by welcoming members back and asking the girls to name one thing they remember from the previous group session.

2. The group facilitator will ask the group members if they have any questions about the group rules.

3. The group facilitator will hand out four index cards with the terms *aggressive, passive, passive-aggressive,* and *assertive.* The group facilitator will divide the girls into triads (if twelve members) and each triad will receive one of the index cards. The triads will be asked to (1) define the term in their own words and (2) list the pros and cons of each approach to conflict. For example, how would they define *passive* and what are the pros and cons of being passive.

4. After the girls have completed both tasks, the group members will reassemble in the larger group and present their definitions and pros and cons lists.

5. The group facilitator will redistribute the Maria and Tara worksheet and discuss the four prompts (bottom of the worksheet) that apply the new terms.

6. The group facilitator will ask the group members to discuss which approaches they use when they are in conflict with another girl and why. The facilitator will encourage the group members to use the terms they have learned (aggressive, passive, passive-aggressive, and assertive). If time permits, it may be helpful at this point to pose questions about why it is difficult to be assertive.

7. The group facilitator will do a go around and ask group members which approach to conflict they would like to use most often and why. The facilitator will ask group members to take mental note of any approaches to conflict that they use between this group session and the next.

Facilitator Notes: The facilitator will want to circulate around the different triads and encourage them to list as many pros and cons as possible. The group members may need to review what pro and con mean. Furthermore, they may need to be encouraged to truly explore pros to aggression and passive-aggressive as the girls may believe they are not supposed to consider these approaches beneficial or positive. However, by exploring the pros of each approach, it provides an opportunity to use critical thinking and consider the consequences of each approach. The girls are able to come to their own conclusions and own their decisions. Interestingly, they will most likely select assertive as the healthiest approach with the best consequences.

Session 5: Weighing the Pros and Cons

1. The group facilitator will begin the group by welcoming members back and asking the girls to do a go around and report on their homework (approach to conflict).

2. The group facilitator will ask the group members if they have any questions about the group rules.

3. The group facilitator will ask for two volunteers who are willing to role-play four different scenarios involving "LeShauna" and "Chrissy." The group leader provides the two girls with a script and asks them to step outside of the room to review each of the four scenarios. (This should take approximately three-five minutes.) While the two girls are preparing for the role-play scenarios, the rest of the group members discuss the terms *aggressive, passive, passive-aggressive,* and *assertive.* "Audience members" will then be given a copy of the script and a LeShauna and Chrissy Worksheet (see Appendix) to record the term that best describes the scenario that they witness.

4. The two "actors" will then role-play the four scenarios while group members silently read along. After each scenario, the audience

members will record the term that best describes the approach to conflict that is portrayed by LeShauna.

5.   The group facilitator will then ask group members to report the different approaches to conflict that match the scenarios.

6.   After redistributing a copy of the Relational Aggression Organizational Map worksheet, the group facilitator will ask the group members to discuss the potential consequences of each approach. Group members will be asked if they see any potential connections between the characteristics on the handout and the potential consequences that are revealed during the discussion.

7.   The group facilitator will conclude by doing a go around and asking the group members to discuss what they would have done if they were LeShauna and why.

Facilitator Notes: It may be helpful to put nametags on LeShauna and Chrissy, as the audience members may be confused about how to characterize the approach to conflict. Typically the girls are ready to share stories relating to the role-played scenario. If they are hesitant to begin a discussion, it may be helpful to ask the group members to discuss what approaches they are mostly like to see in their school, grade, and other places, and why they believe this is so.

Session 6: Assertiveness Revisited

1.   The group facilitator will begin the group by welcoming members back and asking the girls to do a go around and report on what they remember from the previous session.

2.   The group facilitator will ask the group members if they have any questions about the group rules.

3.   The group facilitator will remind the group that there are only five sessions left counting this session before the group will terminate.

4.   The group facilitator will then distribute an Assertiveness Revisited Worksheet (see Appendix). The girls will complete the worksheet independently.

5.   The group facilitator will then pair up the group members and ask them to label each item on the Assertiveness Revisited worksheet as assertive, aggressive, passive, and passive aggressive.

6.   The group facilitator will then go through each item on the worksheet and ask the girls to report on how they labeled each item.

7. The group facilitator will then do a go around and ask each group member to respond to the sentence stem "It is hard to be assertive sometimes because . . . ."

8. The group facilitator will then ask the girls to discuss what they have heard from each other.

9. The group facilitator will ask the girls to discuss how they are learning to be assertive. This may include identifying women they know who they believe demonstrate assertiveness. The group facilitator should contribute to this discussion.

10. To complete the group session, the group facilitator will do a go around and ask each group member to name someone they would like to be assertive with before the next group session.

Facilitator Notes: The facilitator may want to select the pairs so that strong dyads are not put together. Group members should have the opportunity to work with someone in the group that they do not know well. Self-disclosure by the group facilitator may be extremely helpful during this session. Group members may benefit by hearing about why an adult may have difficulty with assertiveness and how the adult is learning to be assertive.

Session 7: How Words Can Hurt or Heal

1. The group facilitator will begin the group by welcoming members back and asking the girls to do a go around and report on who they were assertive with since the last session.

2. The group facilitator will ask the group members if they have any questions about the group rules.

3. The group facilitator will remind the group that there are only four sessions left counting this session before the group will terminate.

4. The group facilitator begins the session by introducing a "paper person"—a life-size paper doll (doll should be made before the session by tracing a person on bulletin board paper). The paper person is taped to the wall or chalkboard, and the group facilitator introduces the paper person as someone who is not liked very much at school.

5. The group facilitator then asks the group what some popular put downs are that are used toward someone they do not like (e.g., *What do people say if they want to pick on paper person?*)

6. A group member is asked to write the insults all over the paper person.

7. Two group members are asked to stand up and verbalize the insults toward the paper person as if they did not like the paper person. After each insult, the group member will rip off a piece of the paper person off.

8. After the paper person is completely ripped down, the group leader then asks the group members to reassemble the paper person using transparent tape.

9. The group facilitator will then draw three columns on the board, labeled *think*, *feel*, and *behave*. The group members then are asked to consider what paper person may think, feel, or do after being "torn down" by others' words. The group facilitator asks the group members to think about whether the paper person's "scars" are symbolic of the scars that real people might have when they are abused by others.

10. The group members are encouraged to talk about what they would say to paper person if she were someone they care about. The group facilitator asks the students to consider these words as healing words that they can use with others.

11. In conclusion, the group members are asked to write a letter to themselves, reminding them of the types of words they want to use with their friends and classmates. If time permits, the group facilitator may ask one or two group members to share their letters with the group.

12. The group will conclude by asking each group member to name someone that they would like to use healing words with prior to the next group session.

Facilitator Notes: The facilitator may need to articulate example insults if group members are hesitant to initiate this aspect of the session. The facilitator will also need to permit enough time for the group members to struggle with reassembling the paper person. Finally, when listing thoughts, feelings, and behaviors, be sure to help group members differentiate between thoughts and feelings.

Session 8: Reflecting on Approaches to Conflict

1. The group facilitator will begin the group by welcoming members back and asking the girls to do a go around and report on what they learned from the last session.

2. The group facilitator will ask the group members if they have any questions about the group rules.

3. The group facilitator will remind the group that there are only three sessions left counting this session before the group will terminate. The group facilitator will also invite group members who have been quiet

during sessions to take a risk and be more active during the Goodwill Girls Game (see Appendix). The sentence stems will need to be cut into strips.

4.   The group facilitator begins the session by showing the group a bowl filled with sentence stems and scenarios. The group facilitator will also hand out an index card that has a large question mark on it to each group member. The bowl will be passed around the group, and group members will pick an item out of the bowl, read it aloud, and respond to the prompt. If group members have a question about the group member's response, they are to raise the index card in the air, and the group member will call on those group members who have questions.

5.   The group facilitator can pass the bowl around the group for as long as time permits.

6.   The group will conclude with the facilitator asking the group members to tell one group member something that she learned from her during the game.

Facilitator Notes: The facilitator should participate as the group may benefit from hearing the facilitator responses to the prompts. Group members enjoy being in control of calling on others, and this process allows them to be assertive in their responses to the questions posed by others.

Session 9: Keep and Toss

1.   The group facilitator will begin the group by welcoming members back and asking the girls to do a go around and name one way being in the group has helped them.

2.   The group facilitator will ask the group members to talk about their thoughts and feelings related to the group ending after the next week's session.

3.   The group facilitator will distribute paper and markers and ask the girls to make two columns on their sheet of paper. At the top of the left-hand column, the girls will write *keep* and at the top of the right-hand column, the girls will write *toss*. The group facilitator will invite the group members to write down friendships behaviors that they do or are learning about in the group that they want to keep and behaviors consistent with relational and social aggression that they would like to toss or not do anymore. Challenge the girls to come up with at least three ideas for each column.

4.   The group facilitator will then give the girls scissors and ask them to cut off the toss column and cut the toss items into individual strips that they will read aloud to the group.

5. After each girl has cut her toss items into strips, the group facilitator will ask for a volunteer to begin tossing her unwanted behaviors into a garbage can that has been placed in the center of the group. As she tosses each item, she will read them aloud to other group members.

6. After the last group member has had to chance to take a turn, the facilitator may self-disclose one example of a change she has made regarding how she negotiates or solves problems with her friends. The group facilitator may also talk about one obstacle that she faced in making this change permanent (e.g., I decided that I needed to assertively confront my friends if I believe that one of them has mistreated me. It is hard sometimes to be honest with how I feel because I worry about my friend getting mad. But I realize that being honest is important if I want to have strong friendships.)

5. The group facilitator can then invite other group members to talk about challenges they face in making these changes.

6. The group will conclude with the facilitator asking the group members to name one person they will go to for help or support if they are having difficulty with their new changes.

Facilitator Notes: The facilitator should only self-disclose if she is comfortable doing so; however, it is important to keep in mind that group members are consistently being asked to be open and honest with the group.

Session 10: Termination

1. The group facilitator will begin the group by welcoming members back and asking the girls if they have any thoughts or feelings about last week's "keep and toss" activity.

2. The group facilitator will ask the girls to talk about what it feels like to participate in the last group session.

3. The group facilitator will ask the group members to write a letter or draw a picture to the group that they will share with the group. This may include what they want the group to know, what the group has meant to them, and so on. The group facilitator should give the group members 10 to 15 minutes to complete this task. Group members will need paper, pens, pencils, and markers or crayons.

4. When everyone is ready, the group members will take turns sharing their letter or picture with the group.

5. The group facilitator should take a turn and talk to the group about the positive changes she has observed, including how the group as a whole has learned to listen to one another and work together on various tasks. The group facilitator may want to consider personal feedback to each group member through a note or card.

6. The group can celebrate their remaining minutes together with food and drink.

Facilitator Notes: Timing is critical. The facilitator needs to plan effectively and make sure that group members have plenty of time to discuss what the termination process is like for them as well as express their gratitude to the group.

CONCLUSION

Group counseling may be an excellent form of intervention for girls and adolescent females at risk for or already participating in relational and social aggression. It is important for counselors to be thoughtful in developing a group-counseling experience by securing permission and support from important stakeholders (e.g., administrators, parents, and teachers) and being organized about group logistics so that group meetings are predictable and occur on a regular basis. Group facilitators must be mindful to keep group members involved and active in discussion throughout the group process so that a psychoeducational group such as this does not simply become "teaching" to a small group of students. As mentioned in Chapter 3, group counseling is one tertiary intervention for relational and social aggression that is focused on awareness and skill development for pubescent or adolescent girls.

Appendix

Handouts for Goodwill Girls
Small-Group Curriculum

UNHEALTHY FRIEND

Puts you down and makes you feel bad about yourself	Tells your secrets to other people	Gives you the silent treatment when she is angry with you
Embarrasses you in public	Is jealous when you spend time with other friends	Tries to control what you do, say, or wear
Always makes decisions for the two of you	Threatens to not be your friend unless you do what she wants	Does not listen to your ideas
Wants you to be honest but then doesn't like when you are	Talks about you behind your back	Fights with you a lot yet doesn't solve the problems with you

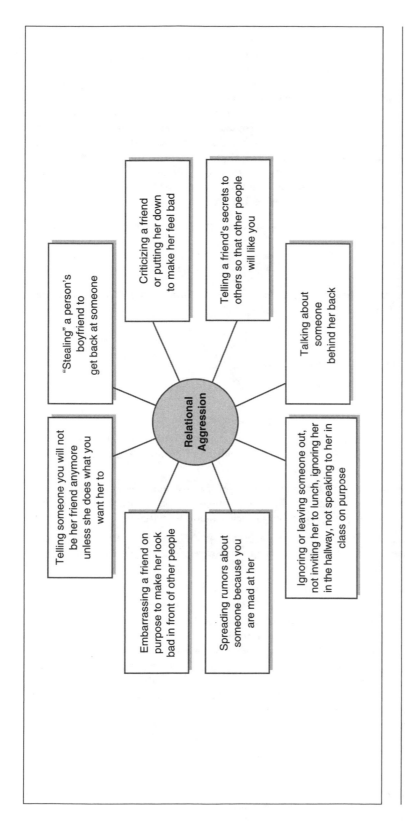

Relational Aggression

"Stealing" a person's boyfriend to get back at someone

Criticizing a friend or putting her down to make her feel bad

Telling a friend's secrets to others so that other people will like you

Telling someone you will not be her friend anymore unless she does what you want her to

Talking about someone behind her back

Embarrassing a friend on purpose to make her look bad in front of other people

Spreading rumors about someone because you are mad at her

Ignoring or leaving someone out, not inviting her to lunch, ignoring her in the hallway, not speaking to her in class on purpose

Maria and Tara are friends in eighth grade at Pitts Middle School. During the weekend, Maria stayed overnight at Tara's house on Friday, and the two girls planned to go to the mall and to a movie on Saturday. While they were getting ready in Tara's bedroom to go to the mall, Maria and Tara started arguing over Maria's outfit. Tara accused Maria of always copying what Tara wore. This hurt Maria's feelings, and she started to get angry. Maria and Tara started arguing and wouldn't stop. Maria accused Tara of being a "snot." Tara accused Maria of being a "baby" who always had to get her way. The argument got so bad that Maria stormed out of the bedroom and asked Tara's father to take her home. Maria told Tara's dad that she didn't want to go to the mall anymore. Tara was very angry after Maria left her house and would not call or IM Maria the next day (Sunday). Tara planned what to do on Monday when they saw each other again before first period.

1. If Tara decides to tell Maria that she does not want to be her friend any more, is this relational aggression?

2. If Tara decides to spread mean rumors about Maria at school, is this relational aggression?

3. What do you think Tara should do?

Aggressive: Being demanding, hostile, rude, and insensitive to the rights of others. People who are aggressive frequently intimidate others into doing what they want and are frequently disrespectful.

Passive Aggressive: Using a combination of passive and aggressive behaviors. Passive-aggressive people typically "show" one thing (being nice) and do another (talk bad about people because they are really angry with them).

Assertive: Being direct, honest, and appropriate while stating one's thoughts, feelings, needs, and wants. Assertive people take care of themselves while simultaneously respecting others.

Passive: Frequently giving in to other's wishes in order to prevent conflict. People who are passive often do not express their thoughts or feelings or stand up for themselves.

1. If Tara decides to yell at Maria in first period in front of everyone, Tara is using a(n) _____ approach to conflict.
2. If Tara tells Maria that she is very sorry and that she will do anything to be her friend again, Tara is using a(n) _____ approach to conflict.

3. If Tara tells Maria that she feels bad about the argument and wishes that she and Tara could talk out their problems without getting so angry, Tara is using a(n) _____ approach to conflict.
4. If Tara apologizes to Maria and then whispers negative things about Maria to their friend Shelly, Tara is using a(n) _____ approach to conflict.

LESHAUNA AND CHRISSY

SCENE 1:

SCENE 2:

SCENE 3:

SCENE 4:

Assertive, Passive, Passive Aggressive, Aggressive

APPROACHES TO CONFLICT

Aggressive: Being demanding, hostile, rude, and insensitive to the rights of others. People who are aggressive frequently intimidate others into doing what they want and are frequently disrespectful.

Passive Aggressive: Using a combination of passive and aggressive behaviors. Passive-aggressive people typically "show" one thing (being nice) and do another (talk badly about people because they are really angry with them).

Assertive: Being direct, honest, and appropriate while stating one's thoughts, feelings, needs, and wants. Assertive people take care of themselves while simultaneously respecting others.

Passive: Frequently giving into others' wishes in order to prevent conflict. People who are passive often do not express their thoughts or feelings or stand up for themselves.

Possible Treasures	Top Five Things I Treasure
Family	1.
Friends	2.
Romantic relationship	3.
Sports	4.
Grades	5.
Future career	
Pets	
Music	
How I look	
Art	
Clubs	
Church	
College education	
Hobbies: _____	
Activities: _____	

I Treasure . . .

References

Andreou, E. (2006). Social preference, perceived popularity, and social intelligence: Relations to overt and relational aggression. *School Psychology International, 27,* 339–351.

Archer, J., & Coyne, S. M. (2005). An integrated review of indirect, relational, and social aggression. *Personality and Social Psychology Review, 9,* 212–230.

Associated Press. (2008, July 1). Missouri: Cyberbullying law is passed. *New York Times,* p. 16.

Bandura. A. (1977). *Social learning theory.* New York: General Learning Press.

Barber, B. K. (1996). Parental psychological control: Revisiting a neglected construct. *Child Development, 67,* 3296–3319.

Bauman, S., & Del Rio, A. (2006). Preservice teachers' responses to bullying scenarios: Comparing physical, verbal, and relational bullying. *Journal of Educational Psychology, 98,* 219–231.

Baumrind, D. (1966). Effects of authoritative parental control on child behavior. *Child Development, 37,* 887–907.

Belgrave, F. Z., Brome, D. R., & Hampton, C. (2000). The contribution of Afrocentric values and racial identity to the prediction of drug knowledge, attitudes, and use among African American youth. *Journal of Black Psychology, 26,* 386–401.

Bloch, D., & Merritt, J. (1993). *Positive self-talk for children: Teaching self-esteem through affirmations.* New York: Bantam.

Boulton, M. J., & Underwood, K. (1992). Bully victim problems among middle school children. *British Journal of Educational Psychology, 62,* 73–87.

Bowen, M. (1978). *Family therapy in clinical practice.* New York: Jason Aronson.

Bowers, L., Smith, P. K., & Binney, V. (1994). Perceived family relationships of bullies, victims, and bully/victims in middle childhood. *Journal of Social and Personal Relationships, 11,* 215–232.

Brazelton, T. B., & Greenspance, S. I. (2000). *The irreducible needs of children: What every child must have to grow, learn, and flourish.* Cambridge, MA: Perseus Publishing.

Brizendine, L. (2006). *The female brain.* New York: Broadway Books.

Brown, L. (2003). *Girlfighting: Betrayal and rejection among girls.* New York: New York University Press.

Brown, S. A., Arnold, D. H., Dobbs, J., & Doctoroff, G. L. (2007). Parenting predictors of relational aggression among Puerto Rican and European

American school-age children. *Early Childhood Research Quarterly, 22,* 147–159.

Bryan, J. H., & Bryan, T. H. (1995). *Amazing discoveries: Social science experiments in the middle school classroom.* Ann Arbor, MI: Exceptional Innovations.

Campbell, J. J., & Frabutt, J. M. (1999, April). *Familial antecedents of children's overt and relational aggression.* Paper presented at the biennial meeting of the Society for Research in Child Development, Albuquerque, NM. (ERIC Document Reproduction Service No. ED430705).

Cappella, E., & Weinstein, R. (2006). The prevention of social aggression among girls. *Social Development, 15,* 434–462.

Casas, J. F., Weigel, S. M., Crick, N. R., Ostrov, J. M., Woods, K. E., Jansen Yeh, E. A., et al. (2006). Early parenting and children's relational and physical aggression in the preschool and home contexts. *Journal of Applied Developmental Psychology, 27,* 209–227.

Casey-Cannon, S., Hayward, C., & Gowen, K. (2001). Middle-school girls' reports of peer victimization: Concerns, consequences, and implications. *Professional School Counseling, 5,* 138–147.

Chesler, P. (2001). *Woman's inhumanity to woman.* New York: Thunder's Mouth Press.

Cole, J. C. M., Cornell, D. G., & Sheras, P. (2006). Identification of school bullies by survey methods. *Professional School Counseling, 9,* 305–313.

Colvin, G., Tobin, T., Beard, K., Hagan, S., & Sprague, J. (1998). The school bully: Assessing the problem, developing interventions, and future research directions. *Journal of Behavioral Education, 8,* 293–319.

Conway, A. M. (2005). Girls, aggression, and emotion regulation. *American Journal of Orthopsychiatry, 75,* 334–339.

Coyne, S. M., Archer, J., & Eslea, M. (2004). Cruel intentions on televisions and in real life: Can viewing indirect aggression increase viewers' subsequent indirect aggression? *Journal of Experimental Child Psychology, 88*(3), 234–253.

Coyne, S. M., Archer, J., & Eslea, M. (2006). We're not friends anymore! Unless . . . : The frequency and harmfulness of indirect, relational, and social aggression. *Aggressive Behavior, 32,* 294–307.

CQ Researcher. (2008). *Growing phenomenon, 18*(17), 394–396.

Craig, W. M. (1998). The relationship among bullying, victimization, depression, anxiety, and aggression in elementary school children. *Personality and Individual Differences, 24,* 123–130.

Crick, N. R. (1996). The role of overt aggression, relational aggression, and prosocial behavior in the prediction of children's future social adjustment. *Child Development, 67,* 2317–2327.

Crick, N. R., Bigbee, M. A., & Howes, C. (1996). Gender differences in children's normative beliefs about aggression: How do I hurt thee? Let me count the ways. *Child Development, 67,* 1003–1114.

Crick, N. R., & Dodge, K. A. (1994). A review and reformulation of social information-processing mechanisms in children's social adjustment. *Psychological Bulletin, 115,* 74–101.

Crick, N. R., & Grotpeter, J. K. (1995). Relational aggression, gender, and social-psychological adjustment. *Child Development, 66,* 710–722.

Crick, N. R., & Grotpeter, J. K. (1996). Children's treatment by peers: Victims of relational and overt aggression. *Development and Psychopathology, 8,* 367–380.

Crick, N. R., & Nelson, D. A. (2002). Relational and physical victimization within friendships: Nobody told me there'd be friends like these. *Journal of Abnormal Child Psychology, 30,* 599–607.

Crick, N. R., Ostrov, J. M., & Werner, N. E. (2006). A longitudinal study of relational aggression, physical aggression, and children's social-psychological adjustment. *Journal of Abnormal Child Psychology, 34,* 131–142.

Crick, N. R., & Werner, N. E. (1998). Response decision processes in relational and overt aggression. *Child Development, 69*(6), 1630–1639.

Crick, N. R., Werner, N., Casas, J., O'Brien, K., Nelson, D., Grotpeter, J., et al. (1999). Childhood aggression and gender: A new look at an old problem. *Gender and Motivation.* Nebraska Symposium on Motivation, 45, Lincoln, NE: University of Nebraska Press.

Crothers, L. M., Field, J. E., & Kolbert, J. B. (2005). Navigating power, control, and being nice: Adolescent girls' friendships. *Journal of Counseling and Development, 83*(3), 349–352.

Crothers, L. M., Field, J. E., Kolbert, J. B., Bell, G. R., Blasik, J. L., Camic, L. A., et al. (2007). Relational aggression in childhood and adolescence: Etiology, characteristics, diagnostic assessment, and treatment. *Counseling and Human Development, 39,* 1–24.

Crothers, L. M., & Levinson, E. M. (2004). Assessment of bullying: A review of methods and instruments. *Journal of Counseling and Development, 82,* 496–503.

Culotta, C. M., & Goldstein, S. E. (2008). Adolescents' aggressive and pro social behavior: Associations with social anxiety and jealousy. *The Journal of Genetic Psychology, 169*(1), 21–33.

de Shazer, S. (1985). *Keys to solutions in brief therapy.* New York: Norton.

Dellasega, C., & Adamshick, P. (2005). Evaluation of a program designed to reduce relational aggression in middle school girls. *Journal of School Violence, 4,* 63–76.

Ellis, A. (2001). *Overcoming destructive beliefs, feelings, and behaviors.* New York: Prometheus Books.

Emmett, J. D., & Monsour, F. (1996). Open classroom meetings: Promoting peaceful schools. *Elementary School Guidance and Counseling, 31,* 3–10.

Eslea, M., Menesini, E., Morita, Y., O'Moore, M, Mora-Merchan, J. A., Pereira, et al. (2003). Friendship and loneliness among bullies and victims: Data from seven countries. *Aggressive Behavior, 30,* 71–83.

Feshbach, N. (1969). Sex differences in children's modes of aggressive responses toward outsiders. *Merrill-Palmer Quarterly, 15,* 249–258.

Field, J. E., Crothers, L. M., & Kolbert, J. B. (2006). Fragile friendships: Exploring the use and effects of indirect aggression among adolescent girls. *Journal of School Counseling, 4.* Retrieved October 24, 2006, from http://www.jsc.montana.edu/articles/v4n5.pdf.

Fraser, M. W., Galinsky, M. J., Smokowski, P. R., Day, S. H., Terzian, M. A., Rose, R. A., et al. (2005). Social information-processing skills training to promote social competence and prevent aggressive behavior in the third grades. *Journal of Consulting and Clinical Psychology, 73*, 1045–1055.

French, D. C., Jansen, E. A., & Pidada, S. (2002). United States and Indonesian children's and adolescent's report of relational aggression by disliked peers. *Child Development, 73*, 1143–1150.

Galen, B. R., & Underwood, M. K. (1997). A developmental investigation of social aggression among children. *Developmental Psychology, 33*, 589–600.

Gilbert, R. M. (1992). *Extraordinary relationships: A new way of thinking about human interaction.* New York: John Wiley & Sons.

Glasser, W. (1969). *Schools without failure.* New York: Harper & Row.

Glover, D., Gough, G., Johnson, M., & Cartwright, N. (2000). Bullying in 25 secondary schools: Incidence, impact, and intervention. *Educational Research, 42*, 141–156.

Goldstein, S. E., & Tisak, M. S. (2004). Adolescents' outcome expectancies about relational aggression within acquaintanceships, friendships, and dating relationships. *Journal of Adolescence, 27*(3), 283–302.

Greene, M. B. (2006). Bullying in schools: A plea for measure of human rights. *Journal of Social Issues, 62*, 63–79.

Gross, J. J., & Levenson, R. W. (1997). Hiding feelings: The acute effects of inhibiting negative and positive emotion. *Journal of Abnormal Psychology, 106*, 95–103.

Grossman, B. G. (2000). *The impact of classroom context on the development of aggression in children.* Unpublished doctoral dissertation, Texas A & M University.

Grotpeter, J. K. (1998). *Relational aggression, overt aggression, and family relationships.* Unpublished doctoral dissertation, University of Illinois at Urbana-Champaign.

Grotpeter, J. K., & Crick, N. R. (1996). Relational aggression, overt aggression, and friendship. *Child Development, 67*, 2328–2338.

Harrist, A. W., & Bradley, K. D. (2003). "You can't say you can't play": Intervening in the process of social exclusion in the kindergarten classroom. *Early Childhood Research Quarterly, 18*, 185–205.

Hart, C. H., Nelson, D. A., Robinson, C. C., Olsen, S. F., & McNeilly-Choque, M. K. (1998). Overt and relational aggression in Russian nursery-school-age children: Parenting style and marital linkages. *Developmental Psychology, 34*, 687–697.

Hayward, S. M., & Fletcher, J. (2003). Relational aggression in an Australian sample: Gender and age differences. *Australian Journal of Psychology, 55*(3), 129–134.

Kohlberg, L. (1976). Moral stages and moralization: The cognitive-developmental approach. In T. Lickona (Ed.), *Moral development and behavior* (pp. 31–53). New York: Holt, Rinehart, & Winston.

LaFontana, K. M., & Cillessen, A. H. N. (2002). Children's perceptions of popular and unpopular peers: A multi-method assessment. *Developmental Psychology, 38*, 635–647.

Lagerspetz, K. M., Björkqvist, K., Berts, M., & King, E. (1982). Group aggression among school children in three schools. *Scandinavian Journal of Psychology, 23*, 45–52.

Lagerspetz, K. M., Björkqvist, K., & Peltonen, T. (1988). Is indirect aggression typical of females? Gender differences in aggressiveness in 11-to-12-year-old children. *Aggressive Behavior, 14*, 403–414.

La Greca, A. M., & Harrison, H. M. (2005). Adolescent peer relations, friendships, and romantic relationships: Do they predict social anxiety and depression? *Journal of Clinical Child and Adolescent Psychology, 34*, 49–61.

Lane, R. D., & Schwartz, G. E. (1998). Levels of emotional awareness: A cognitive-developmental theory and its application to psychopathology. *American Journal of Psychiatry, 144*, 133–143.

Leadbeater, B., Hoglund, W., & Woods, T. (2003). Changing contexts? The effects of a primary prevention program on classroom levels of peer relational and physical victimization. *Journal of Community Psychology, 31*, 397–418.

Letendre, J. (2007). Sugar and spice but not always nice: Gender socialization and its impact on development and maintenance of aggression in adolescent girls. *Child and Adolescent Social Work Journal, 24*(4), 353–368.

Long, C. (2008). Silencing cyberbullies. *NEA Today, 26*(8), 28–29.

Loudin, J. L., Loukas, A., & Robinson, S. (2003). Relational aggression in college students: Examining the roles of social anxiety and empathy. *Aggressive Behavior, 29*, 430–439.

Loukas, A., Paulos, S. K., & Robinson, S. (2005). Early adolescent social and overt aggression: Examining the roles of social anxiety and maternal psychological control. *Journal of Youth and Adolescence, 35*, 335–345.

Lytle, L. J., Bakken, L., & Romig, C. (1997). Adolescent female identity development. *Sex Roles, 37*(3/4), 175–185.

Maslow, A. (1943). A theory of human motivation. *Psychological Review, 50*, 370–396.

Mayeux, L., Underwood, M. K., & Risser, S. D. (2007). Perspectives on the ethics of sociometric research with children: How children, peers, and teachers help inform the debate. *Merrill-Palmer Quarterly, 53*, 53–78.

Merrell, K. W., Buchanan, R., & Tran, O. (2006). Relational aggression in children and adolescents: A review with implications for school settings. *Psychology in the Schools, 43*(3), 345–360.

Mills, R., Freeman, W., Clara, I., Elgar, F., Walling, B., & Mak, L. (2007). Parent proneness to shame and the use of psychological control. *Journal of Child & Family Studies, 16*, 359–374.

Nichols, M. P., & Schwartz, R. C. (2006). *Family therapy: Concepts and methods* (7th ed.). Needham Heights, MA: Allyn and Bacon.

O'Donnell, A. S. (2002). Implementation and evaluation of a treatment program for relational aggression and victimization with preadolescent girls. *Dissertation Abstracts International, 63*, 6-B. (UMI No. 3057543).

Olweus, D. (1993). *Bullying at school: What we know and what we can do.* Malden, MA: Blackwell.

Olweus, D. (2003). A profile of bullying at school. *Educational Leadership 60*(6), 12–17.

O'Neill, A., & Huliska-Beith, L. (2002). *The Recess Queen.* New York: Scholastic Press.

Österman, K., Björkqvist, K., Lagerspetz, K., Kaukiainen, A., Landau, S., Fraczek, A., et al. (1998). Cross cultural evidence of female indirect aggression. *Aggressive Behavior, 24,* 1–8.

Owens, L., Shute, R., & Slee, P. (2000). Guess what I just heard! Indirect aggression among teenage girls in Australia. *Aggressive Behavior, 26,* 67–83.

Owens, L., Slee, P., & Shute, R. (2000). It hurts a hell of a lot . . . : The effects of indirect aggression on teenage girls. *School Psychology International, 21,* 359–376.

Pakaslahti, L., & Keltikangas-Järvinen, L. (2000). Comparison of peer, teacher, and self-assessments on adolescent direct and indirect aggression. *Educational Psychology, 20,* 177–190.

Paquette, J. A., & Underwood, M. K. (1999). Gender differences in young adolescents' experiences of peer victimization: Social and physical aggression. *Merrill-Palmer Quarterly, 45,* 242–266.

Pellegrini, A. D. (1996). *Observing children in their natural worlds: A methodological primer.* Mahwah, NJ: Erlbaum.

Pellegrini, A. D., & Bartini, M. (2000). An empirical comparison of methods of sampling aggression and victimization in school settings. *Journal of Educational Psychology, 92,* 360–366.

Penney, T. L. (2007). *Relational aggression and victimization in early adolescence: Assessing the influence of parenting.* Unpublished doctoral dissertation. University of New Brunswick, Canada.

Piaget, J. (1932). *The moral judgment of the child.* New York: Harcourt Brace Jovanovich.

Piaget, J. (1952). *The origins of intelligence in children.* (M. Cook, Trans.). New York: International Universities Press.

Pipher, M. (1994). *Reviving Ophelia: Saving the selves of adolescent girls.* New York: Ballantine Books.

Prinstein, M. J., Boergers, J., & Vernberg, E. M. (2001). Overt and relational aggression in adolescents: Social-psychological adjustment of aggressors and victims. *Journal of Clinical Child Psychology, 30,* 479–491.

Remillard, A. M., & Lamb, S. (2005). Adolescent girls coping with relational aggression. *Sex Roles, 53,* 221–229.

Richards, J. M., & Gross, J. J. (1999). Composure at any cost? The cognitive consequences of emotion suppression. *Personality and Social Psychology Bulletin, 25,* 1033–1044.

Rigby, K., & Slee, P. T. (1993). Dimensions of interpersonal relation among Australian children and implications for psychological well-being. *Journal of Social Psychology, 133,* 33–42.

Roecker-Phelps, C. E. (2001). Children's responses to overt and relational aggression. *Journal of Clinical Child Psychology, 30,* 240–252.

Sandstrom, M. J. (2007). A link between mothers' disciplinary strategies and children's relational aggression. *British Journal of Developmental Psychology, 25,* 399–407.

Santrock, J. W. (2006). *Life-span development* (11th ed.). New York: McGraw-Hill.

Shechtman, Z. (2002). Aggression and classroom climate: Relations and applications. Paper presented at the annual meeting of the American Psychological Association, Chicago, IL. (ERIC Document Reproduction Service No. 470418).

Shriver, T. P., & Weissberg, R. P. (2005, August 16). No emotion left behind. *New York Times,* p. 15.

Siequeland, L., Kendall, P. C., & Steinberg, L. (1996). Anxiety in children: Perceived family environments and observed family interaction. *Journal of Clinical Child Psychology, 25,* 225–237.

Simmons, R. (2002). *Odd girl out: The hidden culture of aggression in girls.* Orlando, FL: Harcourt.

Skinner, C. H., Cashwell, T. H., & Skinner, A. L. (2000). Increasing tootling: The effects of a peer-monitored group contingency program on students' reports of peers' pro-social behaviors. *Psychology in the Schools, 37,* 263–270.

Smith, P. K., & Sharp, S. (Eds.). (1994). *School bullying: Insights and perspectives.* London: Routledge.

Sramová, B. (2004). Cognitive training—Teacher's help. *Studia Psychological, 46,* 203–210.

Storch, E. A., & Esposito, L. E. (2003). Peer victimization and posttraumatic stress among children. *Child Study Journal, 33,* 91–98.

Sullivan, T. N., Farrell, A. D., & Kliewer, W. (2006). Peer victimization in early adolescence: Associations between physical and relational victimization and drug use, aggression, and delinquent behaviors among urban middle school students. *Development and Psychopathology, 18,* 119–137.

Talbott, E. (1997). Reflecting on antisocial girls and the study of their development: Researchers' views. *Exceptionality, 7,* 267–272.

Taylor, J. M., Gilligan, C., & Sullivan, A. M. (1995). *Between voice and silence: Women and girls, race, and relationship.* Cambridge, MA: Harvard University Press.

Updegraff, K. A., Thayer, S. M., Whiteman, S. D., Denning, D. J., & McHale, S. M. (2005). Relational aggression in adolescents' sibling relationships: Links to sibling and parent-adolescent relationship quality. *Family Relations, 54,* 373–385.

Van Schoiack-Edstrom, L., Frey, K. S., & Beland, K. (2002). Changing adolescents' attitudes about relational and physical aggression: An early evaluation of a school-based intervention. *School Psychology Review, 31,* 201–216.

Vygotsky, L. S. (1962). *Thought and language.* Cambridge, MA: MIT Press.

Weisz, J. R., Suwanlert, S., Chaiyasit, W., Weiss, B., Achenbace, T. M., & Eastman, K. L. (1993). Behavioral and emotional problems among Thai and American adolescents: Parents reports for ages 12–16. *Journal of Abnormal Psychology, 102,* 395–403.

Werner, N. E., & Nixon, C. L. (2005). Normative beliefs and relational aggression: An investigation of the cognitive bases of adolescent aggressive behavior. *Journal of Youth and Adolescence, 34,* 229–243.

Wiseman, R. (2002). *Queenbees and wannabes: Helping your daughter survive cliques, gossip, boyfriends, and other realities of adolescence.* New York: Three Rivers Press.

Wolf, N. (2002). *The beauty myth: How images of beauty are used against women.* New York: Harper Collins.

Wolfradt, U., Hempel, S., & Miles, J. N. V. (2003). Perceived parenting styles, depersonalization, anxiety, and coping behavior in adolescents. *Personality and Individual Differences, 34,* 521–532.

Woods, S., & Wolke, D. (2003). Does the content of anti-bullying policies inform us about the prevalence of direct and relational bullying behavior in primary schools? *Educational Psychology, 23,* 381–401.

Woolfolk, A. (2004). *Educational psychology.* (9th ed.). Boston: Allyn and Bacon.

Xie, H., Farmer, T. W., & Cairns, B. D. (2003). Different forms of aggression among inner-city African American children: Gender, configurations, and school social networks. *Journal of School Psychology, 41,* 355–375.

Xie, H., Swift, D. J., Cairns, B. D., & Cairns, R. B. (2002). Aggressive behaviors in social interaction and developmental adaptation: A narrative analysis of interpersonal conflicts during early adolescence. *Social Development, 11,* 205–224.

Yalom, I., & Leszcz, M. (2005). *The theory and practice of group psychotherapy* (5th ed.). New York: Basic Books.

Yoon, J. S., Barton, E., & Taiariol, J. (2004). Relational aggression in middle school: Educational implications of developmental research. *Journal of Early Adolescence, 24,* 303–318

Young, E. L., Boye, A. E., & Nelson, D. A. (2006). Relational aggression: Understanding, identifying, and responding in schools. *Psychology in the Schools, 43,* 297–312.

Index

CORWIN

A SAGE Company

The Corwin logo—a raven striding across an open book—represents the union of courage and learning. Corwin is committed to improving education for all learners by publishing books and other professional development resources for those serving the field of PreK–12 education. By providing practical, hands-on materials, Corwin continues to carry out the promise of its motto: **"Helping Educators Do Their Work Better."**